Toe Timata le Ūpega

Recasting the Net for a Living Church

Reupena Maulolo

Philip
Garside
Publishing Ltd.

Email Reupena at: reupena.maulolo@gmail.com

Paperback International edition 2025:
ISBN 9781991027986

Also available
New Zealand paperback: ISBN 9781991027979
Paperback print-on-demand USA: ISBN 9798273848122
PDF eBook: ISBN 9781991027993
ePub / Kindle eBook: ISBN 9781067125202

Philip Garside Publishing Ltd
39 Sydenham Street
Northland
Wellington 6012
Aotearoa New Zealand
books@pgpl.co.nz – www.philipgarsidebooks.com

Cover image:
Created by Philip Garside using ChatGPT

Contents

This book is dedicated to my parents

the late Maulolo Faavevela Aiaifua Maulolo
and
the late Pu'a Tausili Seuseu Maulolo

Foreword

From the very beginning of Christian witness, preaching has been a central means of communicating the news of the coming kingdom of God. Jesus himself declares that he was sent for this purpose, 'to preach the kingdom of God' (Luke 4:43). The book of Acts contains many instances of the Apostles preaching the news of the kingdom and of the decisive role of Jesus in bringing that kingdom to fruition. Elsewhere in the New Testament we hear of Timothy being appointed to the task of preaching the message handed on to him by Paul (2 Timothy 4:2). The surrounding verses make clear how important this task of preaching is in order to preserve the truth and integrity of the gospel. Equally important then is that the message of the gospel be preached in ways that can be clearly understood.

What happens then when the language used and the manner of preaching fail to communicate effectively with those who listen? What happens when those gathered to hear the preaching of the Word hear it preached in a language that they cannot easily understand? These are the questions that Reupena Maulolo takes up in this timely and important book. It is timely because, as Reupena's careful research has confirmed, a generation of young Samoan Christians, especially those living outside of Samoa, are finding it increasingly difficult to understand what is proclaimed from the pulpit in the churches they attend.

In the research undertaken for this book, Reupena attended carefully to the stories told by young Samoans. He listened to their frustrations, he heard their stories of disillusionment, and he has taken seriously the advice they gave about how things could be better. Rev Dr Maulolo himself, who is now responsible for teaching the art of preaching at Malua Theological College in Samoa, is uniquely placed to offer guidance and to encourage the changes that are needed if young Samoans are to retain their allegiance to the church and be nourished and inspired once again by the preaching they hear in church. Some young people have departed already, but many remain.

They remain because of loyalty to their families; they remain because they believe still in the God who has come among us in the person of Jesus Christ; they remain because they have caught glimpses here and there of what helpful change could look like.

But time is of the essence. More young people will leave the church if the sermons they hear no longer speak of good news for them. More will leave if the preaching is delivered in language they struggle to understand. There is work to be done in order to bring the changes that are needed so that succeeding generations are enabled to hear and receive the gospel with glad and open hearts.

I hope that the church will receive this book as a gift. It is a gift in two parts. It is the gift, first of all, of the voices of young Samoan Christians who have spoken of their faith but also of their frustrations. We ought to give thanks for their faith. And we ought to honour it by attending to their frustrations. The second part of the gift this book offers to us comes in the form of Reupena's wise advice about how the preaching of the church must change if it is to fulfil its intended purpose.

The purpose of preaching is to proclaim the good news of the coming kingdom of God. It is to nourish and inspire people with the news of the gospel. It is to help people follow faithfully in the footsteps of our Lord and Saviour Jesus Christ. Let us take up the task afresh then, so that the preaching of the church will indeed bear fruit among the generations that are coming along after us.

I am grateful to Reupena for writing this book and warmly commend it to your careful and prayerful reading.

Murray Rae
Professor of Systematic Theology
Theology Head of Programme
University of Otago

Introduction:
Why We Must Cast the Net Again

Toe timata le ūpega

In the rhythms of Samoan life, the phrase *toe timata le ūpega* is well known. Literally meaning "let us cast the net again," it is a proverb used by fisherfolk when their first attempt has come back empty. It speaks to both action and humility. The tide may not have been right. The fish may have moved. The net may need repair. But we do not walk away from the sea in despair. Instead, we regroup. We mend what is torn. We reflect on what we have learned. And then, with wisdom and hope, we cast the net once more.

This book is an invitation to the leaders and members of the Congregational Christian Church Samoa (CCCS) – both in Samoa and in New Zealand – to adopt the posture of *toe timata le ūpega* in our approach to preaching, especially as it relates to young people in our congregations. We are not here to discard the net. We are here to mend it, reweave it, and learn how to use it again in a new and changing sea.

A Church at a Crossroads

The CCCS is a strong church, rooted in centuries of faith, tradition, and communal identity. It has nurtured generations of Samoans in the faith, given leadership to the Pacific, and upheld the values of family, discipline, worship, and obedience to God. Its preaching has historically been powerful – shaped by biblical exegesis, theological training, and a strong cultural framework.

But we now find ourselves at a crossroads.

Across many CCCS congregations, especially in New Zealand, we hear a painful and consistent refrain from youth and young adults: the preaching no longer connects. For some, it is too long, too abstract, or delivered in a language they struggle to understand. For others, it speaks to issues that feel far removed from their lived experience –

offering little guidance for the challenges of growing up biculturally, navigating identity in diaspora, or responding to mental health, peer pressure, racism, or digital life.

Ministers and elders are aware of this drift. Many are deeply committed to the wellbeing of their youth and grieve their gradual disengagement. But too often, the tools they have inherited feel inadequate for the task. They may feel caught between honouring the theological rigour and cultural practices of the CCCS tradition – and responding to a generation who live in a vastly different world.

This is not a failure. It is a moment of truth. A moment when the church must ask hard questions about its future. Because if we do not find ways to preach meaningfully to the next generation, the CCCS risks becoming irrelevant to them – a beautiful canoe left unused on the shore.

The Real Issue Is Not Attention Span

Some critics are quick to blame the youth: "They are distracted," "They are lazy," "They only want entertainment." But this is unfair, and untrue.

Young Samoans – in both Samoa and Aotearoa – are deeply spiritual. They are searching for meaning, belonging, identity, and hope. They are capable of engaging with depth, complexity, and challenge. What they lack is not attention span, but connection. Connection to the message. Connection to the language. Connection to the preacher.

Young people want sermons that are clear, meaningful to their lives, and lead to practical, relevant action or insight. It's important to take seriously the real situations modern Christians face in their everyday lives and communities.

When they say that preaching is "boring," what they often mean is that it feels disconnected from their lives. It does not answer their questions. It does not speak their language – sometimes literally, sometimes metaphorically. It uses illustrations and structures that reflect a world that is no longer theirs. It may lean heavily on obedience and shame, when they are longing for grace and understanding. It may repeat phrases they have heard a thousand times, without ever addressing what it means to be a young Samoan Christian in a world of climate change, digital pressures, casual racism, and shifting cultural expectations.

This is not a call for entertainment. It is a cry for relevance.

The Power and Purpose of Preaching

Preaching is central to worship in the CCCS tradition. It is not a side activity. It is the heart of the service – the moment when Scripture is broken open and the voice of God is discerned. Preaching is a sacred act. It is where the *agaga* (spirit) of the people and the Spirit of God meet. At its best, it nourishes, provokes, awakens, comforts, and calls. It shapes lives.

But when preaching is disconnected from context, it becomes mere performance. When it is not rooted in the lived experience of the hearer, it becomes a monologue, not a conversation. And when it fails to speak into the spaces where identity and spirituality meet – especially for young people – it becomes a closed door rather than an open table.

This book asks: What does preaching look like when it takes the life experience of young Samoans seriously? What does it sound like when it is both biblically faithful and culturally responsive? How can preachers become bridges, rather than barriers, between the Word of God and the youth of today?

Preaching and Identity

To answer these questions, we must first understand the link between preaching and identity. In Samoan cosmology, the soul – *mauli* – resides between the *fatu* (heart) and the *māmā* (lungs). This imagery speaks to the deep interweaving of breath, life, emotion, and spirit. Identity – *fa'asinomaga* – is not just individual, but communal. It is shaped by relationships, responsibilities, and rhythms.

When young people say that the church does not feel like their place, they are not rejecting faith. They are expressing a rupture in *va* – the sacred space between self and other, between youth and elders, between preacher and listener, between their spiritual yearning and the church's response.

Reclaiming preaching as a tool of spiritual formation means reclaiming its power to shape identity – not through shame or guilt, but through connection and grace. It means exploring how *teu le va* (cherishing the sacred space between) can become a homiletical practice. And it means helping young Samoans find their place not only in the pew, but in the story of God.

A Samoan Methodology

This book does not begin with a Western model. It begins with *toe timata le ūpega*. The net is our metaphor and our method. It holds many threads:

- Theological depth
- Cultural identity
- Relational wisdom
- Practical insight
- Empirical data
- Real voices.

This work draws from the voices of ministers, elders, youth, and parents – gathered through interviews, questionnaires, stories, and lived experience. It combines qualitative insight with theological reflection. It uses both Western and Pacific scholarship – but it is rooted in the soil of *fa'aSamoa*.

Each chapter will explore a specific aspect of preaching and its impact on youth spirituality, offering a blend of story, reflection, analysis, and practical guidance. While the tone is conversational, the insights are grounded in deep cultural and theological reflection.

Not a Critique – A Call

It is important to say: this book is not a critique of the CCCS or its ministers. It does not set out to blame or dismantle. Instead, it honours what has been – and gently challenges us to consider what could be.

It is an invitation to look at our own practices with fresh eyes. To sit with the discomfort of change. To listen again to the Spirit who moves through every generation – not just the old ones. And to trust that what has been handed down to us is not a museum piece, but a living tradition, capable of renewal.

Who This Book Is For

This book is written first and foremost for ministers and preachers of the CCCS – those who stand in pulpits, week after week, with the sacred task of proclaiming God's Word. It is also for elders, lay leaders, parents, and anyone who cares about the spiritual formation of youth in Samoan churches.

It is for those who wonder why the young people seem disengaged. It is for those who have tried new approaches but are unsure if they are "allowed." It is for those who feel caught between tradition and innovation. And it is for those who want to honour their culture and faith, while also embracing the real and urgent questions of the next generation.

Ministers in other Pacific churches may also find resonance here. So may those in migrant and bicultural communities, navigating similar tensions between ancestral faith and contemporary expression.

Where We Are Going

The chapters that follow will explore questions such as:

- Why do young people find preaching "boring," and what does that really mean?

- What is the role of language, tone, and delivery in preaching to a bicultural congregation?

- How can preaching address the real-life challenges youth face – including identity, belonging, mental health, and racism?

- What does *va* look like in the pulpit, and how can preachers *teu le va* with youth?

- How can we honour Samoan preaching traditions while also developing new homiletical models?

The goal is not to impose a single model, but to spark a new conversation – one rooted in love for the gospel and love for our people.

A Word to the Youth

Finally, if you are a young reader, or someone who has grown up in the CCCS and felt disconnected from it – this book is for you too. Your voice matters. Your questions matter. Your faith matters. This book exists because of you.

You are not a problem to be solved. You are a gift to be honoured. The church does not belong only to the past. It belongs to you. We are listening. We want to do better. We want to cast the net again – with you, for you, and beside you.

Let Us Begin

In the pages ahead, we will explore, question, lament, and hope. We will be honest about what is broken, and courageous about what is possible. We will hold tightly to our faith, and lightly to our forms. We will cast again.

Toe timata le ūpega.

Let us begin.

1 — Between Cultures: Understanding the Samoan Youth Experience

Toe timata le ūpega begins with understanding the currents we are casting into. To recast the net effectively, we must first know the shape of the sea and the nature of the fish. That is, we must come to know deeply the lived experience of the young people we are trying to reach. In the case of the Congregational Christian Church Samoa (CCCS), this means taking seriously the complex, sometimes painful, sometimes beautiful experience of Samoan youth growing up between two cultures – particularly those living in Aotearoa New Zealand.

Growing Up in Two Worlds

The youth of the CCCS in New Zealand are navigating a reality that differs sharply from that of their parents and grandparents. Many of them were born and raised in Aotearoa. Their schools, social lives, media, and even the language of their thoughts are often in English. Yet their homes, churches, and family systems are steeped in Samoan values, language, and hierarchies. This dual experience can be enriching, but it is often also a source of confusion, pressure, and tension.

A young person might speak English fluently, feel confident in Kiwi social settings, and enjoy the freedoms of Western youth culture, while also being expected to perform well in *fa'alavelave*, submit to elders, attend every church function, and remain fluent in Samoan language and customs. Many live in two worlds that operate by very different rules, and they become skilled cultural navigators – code-switching between expectations and norms depending on whether they are at home, school, or church.

However, code-switching takes its toll. It can lead to fragmentation of identity. Young people may begin to feel that they don't fully belong in either world. Too Samoan to be truly Kiwi; too Kiwi to be truly Samoan. This cultural in-betweenness shapes how they hear sermons, how they relate to the church, and how they understand faith.

Even within their own families, this sense of in-between can create distance. Parents may struggle to understand the pressures their children face, while young people may feel they are letting down their parents by not embracing traditional expectations. The pressure to succeed in school, conform socially, and uphold cultural expectations can lead to anxiety, depression, and a deep yearning to belong somewhere completely.

To close the gap between today's youth and church preaching, it's clear that preaching takes real commitment, effort, and time to truly understand the gospel message. When ministers show that kind of dedication, it helps young people sense and understand God's presence through the sermon.

Language as a Bridge and Barrier

Language is one of the most visible fault lines in this cultural experience. Many CCCS services in New Zealand are still conducted primarily in Samoan. While this affirms cultural identity for elders and first-generation migrants, it often alienates younger members whose grasp of Samoan may be limited or entirely absent. Sermons delivered in Samoan can feel like a foreign language class. Even if the young person understands some words, they may miss the nuance, humour, emotion, and theological depth.

The use of complex Samoan language in church, especially the *gagana faa-matai* (chiefly or oratory speech) used in sermons, has become a problem for many young people.

In interviews and surveys with youth, many said they struggle to engage with preaching that they cannot fully understand. Some sit quietly out of respect. Others tune out. A few stop coming to church altogether. The pain is not just linguistic. It's spiritual. It creates the perception that the gospel is for someone else. That the Word of God is not meant for them.

At the same time, the Samoan language is not just a means of communication. It is a carrier of culture, theology, and identity. To abandon it entirely would be a loss. So the challenge becomes: how can preaching hold both languages with care? How can we create bilingual worship that honours heritage while welcoming the present and future generations?

There is also an emotional dimension to language. When sermons are only in Samoan, they may carry tones, cadences, and metaphors that connect powerfully for elders but miss the mark for youth. Language is deeply tied to emotion and experience. If young people cannot access the emotional resonance of a sermon, they may feel uninvited to the heart of worship.

Bilingualism is not merely about translation; it's about transformation. A truly bilingual preaching approach listens first to the lives of the people and then speaks with clarity, courage, and care into both cultural realities.

Cultural Expectations and the Weight of Honour

Young Samoans are also navigating powerful cultural expectations around honour, obedience, and service. In Samoan culture, the value of *fa'aaloalo* (respect) is central. Children are expected to honour their parents, elders, and church leaders. This cultural code, while beautiful in many respects, can sometimes silence genuine questions or struggles. A young person who is wrestling with doubt, sexuality, mental health, or cultural identity may feel unable to speak up for fear of dishonouring their family or church.

This silence can lead to internalised conflict. Youth learn to perform obedience on the outside while hiding their questions and pain on the inside. Preaching that focuses heavily on duty, sin, or condemnation without pastoral sensitivity can compound this pain. It may feel like a rebuke rather than an invitation. It may drive young people further into isolation.

We must remember that respect cannot be forced. It is earned through trust and relationship. In a multicultural, postcolonial context like Aotearoa, where young people are constantly encouraged to question and express themselves, preaching must avoid becoming a voice of control. Instead, it should offer guidance, hope, and pathways to spiritual exploration grounded in grace and truth.

A new model of relational respect is needed – one that maintains the beauty of *faʻaaloalo* but removes its silencing edges. Preachers can model this by honouring youth voices in the pulpit, preaching with vulnerability and honesty, and encouraging open dialogue in safe settings.

Generational Misunderstandings

Another major challenge is the generational gap. Many CCCS elders and ministers grew up in Samoa, trained in traditional methods, and hold firm views on what church should look like. Their experience of faith is shaped by sacrifice, reverence, formality, and long sermons rooted in classic theological models.

In contrast, many youth value authenticity, conversation, short-form communication, visual learning, and emotional resonance. They are not necessarily less spiritual. But the way they engage with faith is different. This can lead to misunderstandings: elders may see youth as disinterested or rebellious, while youth may see elders as out of touch or authoritarian.

One young person described it this way: "When I hear preaching in church, it feels like it's for the adults. Like we're just meant to sit there and absorb it. But it doesn't feel like it sees us."

This is a profound insight. Preaching, in its best form, is a relational act. It must see the people it is addressing. It must acknowledge their reality, speak into their hopes and fears, and offer a word that builds connection and calls forth transformation.

The generational divide can be bridged with intentionality. Preachers can seek out feedback from youth, invite them into worship planning, use their stories as sermon illustrations (with permission), and include youth leaders as co-preachers or discussion facilitators.

Mentoring relationships between elders and youth, structured around mutual listening and theological dialogue, can also help bridge this divide. Elders have wisdom to offer, but they must be willing to receive the wisdom of youth in return.

Preaching That Speaks Into Two Worlds

From a theological point of view, John Stott believes that preaching is a way for God to share divine truth through the preacher, but the focus should always be on God, not the preacher. This means both the preacher and the congregation need to engage in an ongoing conversation about God – that's the real purpose of preaching.

For preaching to be effective for Samoan youth in New Zealand, it must be contextual. It must speak both Samoan and English, literally and metaphorically. It must draw from the richness of Samoan tradition and the immediacy of young people's daily lives. It must name and affirm the bicultural reality of youth, not as a problem but as a gift.

This means shifting how sermons are structured and delivered. It may mean shorter sermons with clearer main points. It may involve storytelling, visuals, or metaphors drawn from Kiwi and Pacific youth culture. It may mean creating interactive or dialogical moments, rather than monologues. It may mean preachers need to listen more – asking youth what they want to hear about, and what they are facing.

In other words, both the preacher and the listeners share responsibility in fulfilling God's purpose. This makes sense today if we understand God's Word as alive and meant to be shared between people through preaching.

Above all, it means preaching with *alofa* (love) that is not sentimental, but bold. Love that names injustice. Love that calls forth hope. Love that bridges the space between pulpit and pew, between generations, between Samoa and New Zealand.

Cultural theologians remind us that contextual preaching does not mean diluting the gospel, but discovering its fresh voice in a new setting. This requires imagination, risk, and trust in the Spirit of God who speaks in many languages.

Tui Atua Tupua Tamasese Efi says that culture connects people and communities with the life of the church, shaping and guiding everything we do. It not only keeps our shared identity alive but also helps the church to grow both spiritually and practically.

Theology of Belonging

One of the deepest needs among Samoan youth is the need to belong. Not just to a family, but to a church community that sees them, values them, and invites them to participate fully. Preaching has a powerful role to play in shaping that sense of belonging.

When young people hear themselves reflected in sermons – when their language, struggles, hopes, and context are named with compassion – they begin to believe that the gospel is for them too. They begin to see the church not as their parents' space, but as their space. They begin to consider faith not as a duty, but as a source of strength and joy.

This requires a theology of hospitality. A vision of God who welcomes, who listens, who journeys with the questioning and the unsure. It requires preachers to shift from being experts delivering truth from on high, to being *fa'afeagaiga* (sacred partners) walking alongside the flock.

The theology of *teu le va* (cherishing the relational space) becomes particularly important here. Preaching becomes not just speech, but a sacred act of maintaining and nurturing the space between people, between generations, and between God and humanity.

Preaching in this light is a sacrament of presence. It says to the youth: "You are here. You are seen. You are needed. God is with you."

Preaching isn't meant to be a way to fix human problems or meet our personal or social needs. God's Word speaks to us with power, cutting through our assumptions and challenging our self-focused idea of freedom.

A Call to Courage and Creativity

If the CCCS is to thrive in New Zealand, it must find the courage to adapt. This does not mean discarding its heritage. Rather, it means finding new vessels to carry ancient truths. Preaching is one such vessel. When preaching is vibrant, inclusive, and honest, it can transform lives.

The church must give permission – theological, cultural, and structural – for new forms of preaching to emerge. Youth must be allowed to preach. Women must be empowered to share the Word.

Lay leaders must be equipped. Elders must be willing to experiment. Ministers must be trained in cross-cultural communication, youth psychology, and creative homiletics.

Training programmes can include youth-led workshops on how to speak across generations. Sermon feedback groups can include people of all ages. Technology can be embraced to share sermons in visual, audio, and digital forms.

Above all, the church must become a community of mutual learning. This is not about fixing youth, but about walking with them – and letting them walk with us.

Conclusion: Listening Before Preaching

If there is one action the CCCS must take before revising sermons, revising theology, or revising language, it is this: we must listen. We must sit down with our youth and ask them about their lives, their dreams, their fears. We must create safe spaces for honesty. We must invite them into leadership, not as token gestures, but as true contributors to the future of the church.

Only then can our preaching speak into both cultures. Only then can our messages carry the weight of truth and the warmth of grace. Only then will the net be strong enough to hold them.

Toe timata le ūpega. Let us begin again – with ears to hear, hearts to feel, and words that bind us together in love.

2 — The Voice from the Pulpit: Why Preaching Still Matters

In every CCCS service, the moment of preaching is sacred. The preacher should understand what's happening in people's lives, but their main concern is how each person stands before God. The preacher ascends to the pulpit, opens the Bible, and begins to speak. For generations, this act has stood as the heart of worship, the place where God's Word is proclaimed to the gathered faithful.

For many young people today – especially those living between Samoan culture and New Zealand life – preaching doesn't carry the same importance it once did. Too often, what they hear from the pulpit feels out of touch with their lives, doesn't speak to their real struggles, or just goes on too long to hold their attention.

This chapter is about reclaiming preaching as a life-giving, relational, and spiritually rich practice. It is not enough to preach out of habit or duty. If preaching is to speak to a new generation, it must come alive again. It must connect. It must matter.

Reclaiming Preaching as Life-Giving

Preaching is not simply about delivering information. At its best, it is an act of creation, a sacred weaving of Scripture, Spirit, and story. It brings to life the ancient Word in the present moment. When preaching is done well, people don't just hear the gospel – they encounter it. They feel known, stirred, challenged, comforted, awakened.

But when preaching becomes a ritual without relevance, a tradition without heart, it begins to wither. Many CCCS youth have described sermons as boring. This is not a criticism of Scripture. It is a longing for connection. The issue is not that the Bible no longer speaks. It is that we must learn again how to listen, and how to speak its truth in the voice of today's people.

We must remember: preaching is not a monologue. It is a conversation. It is a relationship. And relationships require attention, context, and care.

Preaching as Relationship

Preaching is not just about what is said, but who is speaking, and to whom. There are at least three relationships that intersect in every sermon:

1. The Preacher and the Listener

The preacher must know the people. This is foundational in Samoan culture, where communal identity and respect shape every interaction. A preacher who does not understand the lives, languages, and struggles of youth in New Zealand is speaking into a void. The words may be eloquent, but if they do not speak to the heart, they fall flat.

Youth today face complex realities – from identity struggles, to mental health pressures, to the challenges of navigating bicultural life. They need to hear sermons that name these things, sermons that validate their questions, celebrate their strengths, and challenge them with hope. This cannot happen if preaching is only about biblical exposition and not about relationship.

To develop this relationship, preachers must be present beyond the pulpit. They must be in conversation with youth, attending their events, understanding their music, and speaking their language. This requires effort, but it is holy effort – a ministry of presence that builds credibility long before the sermon is preached.

2. The Word and the World

Every good sermon brings Scripture into dialogue with the world. This does not mean watering down the Bible to suit modern tastes. It means taking seriously the call to interpret the Word in ways that speak into real-life context. When Jesus taught, he used stories of farming, fishing, family, and feast. He began where people were, then led them somewhere deeper.

For CCCS youth navigating racism, economic struggle, intergenerational tension, and shifting cultural expectations, the Word must be preached as a lamp to their feet, not an abstract doctrine. It must name their world. This includes drawing on Samoan proverbs, contemporary stories, Pacific issues, and New Zealand youth culture. Only then will the sermon feel like it is for them.

3. God and the Heart

Ultimately, preaching is about encounter. Through the Spirit, the sermon becomes a space where the listener meets the living God. This is not the result of human eloquence but of spiritual attentiveness. The preacher is a vessel, not a performer. And the measure of a good sermon is not applause, but transformation.

To preach well is to prepare in prayer, to listen before speaking, to walk humbly with the text and the people. It is to trust that God still speaks, and that our task is to tune our voices to that frequency. Every preacher must ask not only "what shall I say?" but "what does God want to say – through me – to these people, here and now?"

Preaching and Samoan Identity

In Samoan culture, the spoken word carries deep weight. Oratory is art. Ceremonial speech is sacred. A well-given speech can restore peace, affirm identity, and preserve community. This cultural reverence for language must be reclaimed in the pulpit. Preaching is not just religious talk. It is a form of *faʻalogo* – deep listening and honouring.

This insight invites a shift: from preaching as content delivery to preaching as identity formation. When youth hear sermons that speak into their cultural pride, their personal story, and their ancestral legacy, they feel grounded. They are reminded that their faith is not foreign. It is deeply Samoan. It is deeply theirs.

Too often, our youth feel that church is where their Samoan identity is judged, not embraced. They are expected to conform to a model that may not reflect their real-world experience. But the pulpit can be a place of reclamation. It can say: your bilingual tongue is a gift. Your hybrid identity is holy. Your questions are part of faith.

This is not about pandering. It is about truth-telling. It is about lifting up a theology that celebrates migration, adaptation, resilience, and bicultural wisdom. It is about preaching that reclaims Samoan identity not as something to leave behind for faith, but something that enriches it.

Preaching can also acknowledge and celebrate the *va* – the sacred relational space – between generations. When ministers model respect, listening, and hospitality to the concerns of youth, they model the very message they preach. Preaching becomes a relational bridge, not a wall.

Theological Grounding: Why Preaching Matters

Theologically, preaching is central to the life of the church because it proclaims the Word made flesh. It is through preaching that the gospel is shared, interpreted, and embodied. The Apostle Paul writes, "How can they believe in the one of whom they have not heard? And how can they hear without someone preaching to them?" (Romans 10:14).

John Stott describes preaching as "opening up the inspired text with such faithfulness and sensitivity that God's voice is heard and God's people obey him." This is not about performance or intellect, but faithful witness. Preaching is an act of trust: trust in the Spirit, trust in the Word, and trust in the power of relationship.

Jay Adams speaks of nine convictions that must undergird biblical preaching, including the belief that preaching is God's primary means of communicating his truth, and that it must be faithful, clear, and directed toward transformation.

In the CCCS context, preaching has often been seen as a duty of authority – a sacred responsibility handed down through theological training. But what if we reframed preaching not only as duty, but as *tautua* – service? What if preaching became a form of humble offering, of relationship-building, of cultural celebration?

To preach in this spirit is to follow the model of Christ – who did not lord over his disciples but walked with them, ate with them, and taught them through stories. He spoke plainly, yet powerfully. He met people where they were, then called them deeper. He challenged tradition when it hindered love. He preached not only with words but with his life.

Making the Shift: From Tradition to Transformation

There is no need to abandon traditional preaching. But it must be renewed. This means:

- **Shortening sermons** so that young people can stay engaged without being overwhelmed.

- **Speaking bilingually or contextually**, honouring both Samoan and English, and the lived language of the youth.

- **Using real-life examples** that reflect the world youth live in: school, work, family pressure, friendships, digital culture.

- **Asking questions** rather than giving all the answers. Let sermons invite reflection, not just compliance.

- **Including youth in the preaching process**, whether through testimonies, storytelling, or discussion before the sermon is written.

- **Reframing biblical characters** as relatable figures who also struggled, doubted, or led change.

- **Embedding cultural narratives and values**, such as the Samoan proverbs, metaphors, and ancestral wisdom that link faith to *fa'aSamoa*.

- **Building a team preaching model**, where younger preachers or lay voices are included alongside ordained ministers to increase diversity and connection.

- **Recording and sharing sermons online**, especially in bilingual format, to reach diaspora youth who may not attend regularly.

- **Evaluating impact**, by inviting feedback, testimonies, and dialogue about how sermons are being received and lived.

Preaching will not save the church on its own. But preaching can be a catalyst. It can reopen hearts that have closed. It can reweave the net. It can call the young back not with guilt, but with grace.

To help this happen, preaching must not only inform – it must transform. It must be beautiful. It must be bold. It must be soaked in the language of love, justice, healing, and hope.

Preaching for a Future Church

The task of preaching in the CCCS today is not simply to repeat what has been said before. It is to look ahead, to speak into the future, to dare to imagine a church where youth do not merely attend but lead, speak, and shape the message.

This requires courage – the courage to be vulnerable, to admit when preaching has not connected, and to try again. It also requires humility – to listen well, to learn from others, and to accept that the Spirit moves in new ways through new voices.

Preachers must become cultural interpreters, not just biblical ones. They must stand at the intersection of tradition and transformation, holding space for both ancestral faith and emerging hope. This is not easy. But it is holy work.

To equip this future, CCCS must invest in training and mentorship. Young leaders must be taught not only theology but communication. They need space to practise, to fail, to be heard. We must create preaching labs, peer circles, and bilingual homiletics courses that develop the next generation of CCCS voices.

Conclusion: A Voice That Calls, A Net That Holds

To preach is to love. It is to gather the scattered, speak into silence, and proclaim a God who still walks among us. When we reclaim preaching as a relational, culturally grounded, Spirit-filled practice, we make space for youth to hear the gospel anew.

Let us cast the net again. Let us raise our voices not as echoes of the past, but as heralds of the living Word. For the church to live, its preaching must live. And for preaching to live, it must listen, love, and speak the truth with courage and care.

3 — Why Youth Say Preaching Is Boring: And What That Tells Us

In the many interviews and youth gatherings that informed this research, one phrase came up time and again: "Preaching is boring." This blunt assessment, repeated with weary frustration or quiet disappointment, was not just a critique of style or content. It was a cry for relevance. A signal that something central to worship – the proclamation of the Word – was failing to connect with some of the very people it most urgently needs to reach.

This chapter unpacks that sentiment. It is not an attack on preachers or preaching, but an honest examination of why so many young people in CCCS congregations feel disconnected from the sermons they hear. It explores what "boring" really means in this context, what it reveals about generational expectations, and how the pulpit can become a place of renewal rather than retreat.

Naming the Disconnect

When youth describe preaching as boring, they are not rejecting Scripture. Most hold a deep respect for the Bible. Nor are they rejecting the idea of being challenged, inspired, or taught. What they are rejecting is preaching that feels like it speaks past them instead of to them – sermons that use language they don't understand, that address issues they don't face, and that seem more about religious performance than authentic connection.

The problem is often one of relevance. Many young people say that sermons don't reflect their lived realities. Their struggles with identity, racism, mental health, family pressure, and belonging are rarely mentioned. Instead, the preaching can feel stuck in another time, another place, another generation's concerns.

One young person put it this way: "I want church to be the place where I hear something real – something that helps me get through the week. But sometimes I feel like the preacher is talking to someone else, not me." That feeling – of absence in presence – is more than boredom. It is disconnection. And disconnection, if it continues, becomes disengagement.

The Language Barrier

One of the most immediate obstacles is language. Many youth born or raised in New Zealand are not fluent in Samoan. They understand some phrases, pick up the general tone, but cannot fully grasp the nuance or depth of a Samoan-language sermon. This linguistic gap is compounded by a cultural one: even when English is used, it is often delivered in formal tones or complex theological language that is difficult to access.

For these youth, attending a CCCS service can feel like being at a family event where they are both included and excluded – welcome in the room, but not fully part of the conversation. The sermon, instead of being a bridge, becomes a barrier.

And this is painful. It signals that their version of Samoan identity is somehow incomplete. They are made to feel deficient for not being fluent, rather than affirmed for navigating two cultures. It is no wonder that some tune out or stay away.

At the same time, some youth who do speak Samoan fluently still report a disconnect. The issue is not only about language but about tone, imagery, and focus. Sermons that rely heavily on cultural references unfamiliar to younger generations can leave them confused or disengaged. What is needed is not simply translation, but transformation – a style of preaching that truly takes the bicultural and bilingual reality of young Samoans in Aotearoa seriously.

Generational Expectations

There is also a fundamental difference in what older and younger generations expect from a sermon. For many older members, especially those born in Samoa, preaching is a sacred performance. It is meant to be long, poetic, filled with biblical references, and delivered with rhetorical authority. It reflects respect for tradition and reverence for the preacher's role.

Younger people, on the other hand, often look for clarity, brevity, and authenticity. They value preaching that is conversational, story-based, and emotionally honest. They respond to vulnerability and humour more than to formality and structure. They want to hear how Scripture speaks into their reality – not just what it meant in ancient times, but what it means for their lives now.

This generational mismatch can lead to frustration on both sides. Elders may view youth as disrespectful or spiritually lazy. Youth may view elders as out of touch or controlling. Preaching becomes one more site of tension rather than transformation.

In fact, several young people expressed how they felt guilty for not enjoying sermons – as if their boredom was a spiritual failure, not a systemic problem. This internalised shame can discourage further engagement. It becomes a cycle: youth feel disengaged, then guilty, then less likely to attend, which reinforces elders' perceptions that youth lack commitment.

Tone, Delivery, and Style

Another frequent criticism is the tone and delivery of preaching. Some youth describe it as overly loud, monotone, or emotionally distant. They feel preached at, not spoken with. The preacher's tone can sometimes feel angry or moralistic, especially when addressing issues of behaviour, gender, or church participation.

Many youth long for a different kind of tone – one that feels like an invitation rather than a judgment. They want sermons that speak to them, not about them. They want to hear hope, not just correction; love, not just law.

The length of sermons is also a factor. In an age of short-form content and digital attention spans, a 40-minute sermon with no engagement or interaction can feel punishing. It's not that youth can't concentrate – they can spend hours on a meaningful podcast or YouTube series – but they need to be drawn in, not lectured at.

Some of the most well-received sermons among youth were shorter, more interactive, or included moments of dialogue or reflection. Even simple adjustments – like pausing to ask a question, using multimedia, or incorporating youth voices – can shift the energy in the room.

Being Faithful and Being Real

Some preachers worry that adapting preaching to better connect with youth means watering down the gospel. But relevance is not the enemy of faithfulness. In fact, Scripture itself shows constant adaptation to context. Paul preached differently to Jewish audiences than he did to Greeks. Jesus told different stories to different crowds. The message remained true, but the method shifted.

Preaching can be both biblically grounded and culturally aware. It can speak the truth of God's love, justice, and grace while also naming the everyday realities of life in Aotearoa. It can draw from the richness of Samoan metaphor and proverb while also speaking in the idioms of youth culture.

Being faithful to Scripture means being faithful to its intent: to reveal God's heart to God's people. And God's heart, throughout the Bible, is profoundly relational, dynamic, and concerned with the present moment.

As one youth said, "I don't need the preacher to tell me everything is fine. I need them to tell me how God is with me when it's not." That desire – for realism, not denial – is a profound invitation to preachers.

Listening as the First Step

If youth say preaching is boring, the most faithful response is not to defend the sermon, but to listen to the listener. What are they telling us? What do they long for? What are the sermons that have spoken to them? Who are the preachers they respect, and why?

In many of the interviews, youth said they paid attention when the preacher told a personal story, used humour, or admitted their own struggles. They listened when the sermon connected Scripture to things they cared about: family, future, mental health, cultural pride, justice. They leaned in when the preacher spoke with respect rather than superiority.

This tells us that young people are not disengaged from faith. They are hungry for authenticity. They are waiting for the church to speak a word that matters.

In some cases, youth said they returned to church specifically because of one sermon or preacher who "got it." This highlights the potential impact of even small shifts in preaching. A single sermon can change a trajectory.

Youth Voices Matter

Another common thread is that youth want to participate, not just observe. They want a chance to share their thoughts, their testimonies, their readings of Scripture. Many feel they are talked about in sermons, but rarely heard.

Some churches have begun to respond by creating youth-led services or giving young people opportunities to preach or lead devotions. These moments are often powerful and deeply moving. Youth bring a fresh voice, a different lens, a raw honesty that many adults find inspiring.

But this must go deeper. Youth should not be tokenised. They should be mentored, trained, and trusted. Their insights should shape not just youth services, but the preaching calendar, the theological emphases, and the leadership of the church. When youth shape the pulpit, they begin to trust the pulpit again.

A few CCCS congregations have even experimented with sermon feedback groups – where youth can reflect on and respond to the sermon, offering their thoughts to the preacher or leadership. Such practices not only empower young people but make preaching a communal act of discernment.

What Makes Preaching Come Alive?

So what kind of preaching do youth say they want? Based on interviews, reflections, and observations, several themes emerge:

- **Preaching that tells stories** – Biblical stories, personal testimonies, cultural narratives, and real-life experiences.

- **Preaching that is honest** – That names doubt, struggle, and complexity.

- **Preaching that is relevant** – That connects Scripture to school, work, racism, identity, social media, and the issues youth care about.

- **Preaching that is shorter but deeper** – That respects their time and intelligence.

- **Preaching that is inclusive** – That uses both Samoan and English, that honours diverse identities, that avoids shaming or stereotyping.

- **Preaching that invites response** – That ends with a challenge or question, not just a conclusion.

- **Preaching that feels like a conversation** – That is warm, welcoming, and relational.

When preaching feels like this, youth lean in. They remember it. They talk about it. They come back.

A Church That Speaks With, Not Over

Ultimately, the cry that preaching is boring is a call for transformation, not entertainment. Youth do not want flashy preachers. They want real ones. They want sermons that help them live. They want to know that God sees them, knows them, and has something to say to them.

This will require change. Not all preachers will find it easy. Some will need to unlearn habits, take feedback, and embrace new forms. But the future of the CCCS depends on this willingness. If preaching remains a monologue from the past, it will lose its audience. But if preaching becomes a dialogue with the present, it can change lives.

Let the pulpit be a place of meeting, not dividing. Let it echo not only with tradition but with truth. And let it be filled again with the voices of all God's people – young and old, fluent and learning, questioning and believing, waiting to hear a Word that speaks.

4 — *Teu le Va*:
Tending the Sacred Space Between Us

In Samoan thought, few concepts are as rich and complex as *va*. It is a word that defies direct translation, often rendered as "relational space," yet it carries much more: a sense of sacredness, responsibility, and mutuality. *Teu le va* – to tend or cherish the *va* – is not merely a social nicety. It is a moral and spiritual imperative. It defines the way people relate not only to one another, but to God, the land, the church, and all creation. In the context of preaching, *va* has profound implications for how the pulpit relates to the people, and how the Word of God is mediated through human relationships.

This chapter explores how the principle of *teu le va* can reshape preaching practice within the Congregational Christian Church Samoa (CCCS). It draws from theology, Samoan cultural wisdom, and feedback from youth to examine how preaching can either fracture or restore relationships. In an age of disconnection and disillusionment, especially among younger members, reclaiming the sacredness of *va* may offer a path towards healing and revitalisation.

Understanding *Va:* A Sacred Relational Ethic

At its heart, *va* is about space – not empty space, but the space between people, imbued with meaning. It is relational space: the invisible yet deeply felt connection that links individuals, families, communities, and the divine. In Western thought, space is often something to be filled or crossed. In Samoan thinking, space is something to be honoured.

Va is shaped by *fa'aaloalo* (respect), *alofa* (love), *fa'amalūlū* (humility), and *tausi le vā* (guarding and nurturing that relationship). These principles govern interactions in families, villages, and church life. When the *va* is strong, there is harmony. When the *va* is violated – through disrespect, harsh speech, exclusion, or neglect – the relational fabric is torn. Healing the *va* requires intentional acts of restoration, not just apology, but *tausia* – sustained tending.

In Samoan theology, this extends to the divine-human relationship. God is not a distant being but is known in relationship – in the *va* between Creator and creation, between Word and world. Jesus himself is seen as the perfect *teu le va* – tending the relational space between God and humanity, between Jew and Gentile, between the holy and the everyday.

The Preacher's Role in the *Va*

Preaching is not just the delivery of a message. It is a relational act. The preacher steps into the sacred space between the Word and the people, speaking not only about God but on behalf of God – and simultaneously to the people and with them. This is a weighty calling. It demands more than theological knowledge or rhetorical skill. It demands relational wisdom.

The preacher must first tend their *va* with God. This includes prayer, humility, confession, and openness to the Spirit. But they must also tend their *va* with the congregation – not only with elders and leaders, but with youth, children, those on the margins. If the preacher is emotionally distant, harsh, or condescending, that *va* is damaged, and the sermon, no matter how sound, will not land.

As one young person shared in an interview, "Sometimes I feel like the preacher is shouting over us, not talking with us. It feels like they don't even know we're there." That is a broken *va*. The challenge is not just to preach well, but to preach with awareness – to honour the relational space between pulpit and pew.

Preaching as Healing the *Va*

In many CCCS contexts, preaching has become highly formalised. The pulpit can feel elevated – literally and symbolically – from the people. Preachers are often seen as authority figures rather than fellow journeyers. While respect for the preacher is culturally important, this dynamic can inadvertently widen the gap between generations, especially when youth feel unseen or unheard.

But preaching has the power to heal the *va*. When a preacher speaks with vulnerability, when they tell stories that connect with everyday life, when they acknowledge pain or ask hard questions –

the *va* is strengthened. It becomes a place of mutual recognition, not just of doctrinal instruction.

For example, a sermon that explores mental health, grief, or identity – and does so with compassion – can bridge the gap between young listeners and the church. It says, "We see you. You are not alone." In this way, preaching becomes not just proclamation, but pastoral care. It becomes an act of tending.

This does not mean abandoning theology or compromising truth. On the contrary, the truth of Scripture is best revealed in relationships that honour *va*. Jesus' own preaching was deeply relational – sitting with outcasts, sharing meals, asking questions, meeting people where they were. His words healed because they were spoken within relationship.

Va Between Generations

Nowhere is the need for *teu le va* more evident than in the generational divide within many CCCS congregations. Elders often value tradition, hierarchy, and formality. Youth often value authenticity, participation, and relevance. Both are valid. But when either group dismisses the other, the *va* suffers.

Preaching must therefore become a bridge between generations. This requires preachers to listen to youth, understand their context, and honour their experiences – not as a concession, but as an expression of theological integrity. If God is present in all generations, then preaching must reflect that truth.

A sermon that uses both Samoan and English, that references Scripture and social media, that draws from *fa'aSamoa* and life in Aotearoa – such a sermon tends the *va*. It brings generations into dialogue, not competition.

Preachers might consider including youth voices in their preparation – through conversation, surveys, or collaboration. This act alone strengthens the *va*, making the sermon a shared work of meaning.

Preaching and the *Va* with God

Finally, preaching tends the *va* between people and God. It is a spiritual practice – not a performance. A sermon is not just about conveying information or exhorting behaviour. It is about revealing God's presence in the midst of life.

When preaching is moralistic or fear-based, it can distort the *va* with God – making God seem distant, angry, or controlling. Youth especially report feeling alienated when sermons are focused only on sin, punishment, or obedience, without grace or relationship.

By contrast, when preaching is rooted in love, mercy, and justice, it draws listeners closer to God. It reaffirms that God is not only holy but near. That faith is not only duty but gift. That God desires relationship, not just rule-following. In this way, the *va* is not only maintained but made sacred again.

Practical Ways to Tend the *Va* in Preaching

If *va* is to be more than a concept – if it is to shape preaching practice – then preachers must develop habits that tend the relational space:

- **Spend time with the people** – not just leaders, but youth, families, and those on the margins. Know their stories.

- **Preach with both authority and humility** – authority rooted in Scripture, humility rooted in shared humanity.

- **Use language that invites** – consider tone, pace, and the accessibility of your words.

- **Include Samoan and English** – honour both tongues, without shaming those who struggle.

- **Invite feedback** – not to be defensive, but to listen with love.

- **Pray for your hearers** – not just in preparation, but as a rhythm of ministry.

- **Model relationship from the pulpit** – acknowledge the presence of different age groups, affirm shared journeys.

- **Create space in worship for response** – not only listening, but speaking back, whether through testimony, prayer, or dialogue.

- **Recognise the sermon as part of a wider relationship** – built through pastoral visits, fellowship, mentoring, and service.

- **Practice confession and reconciliation when needed** – if harm has been caused, seek healing of the *va*.

Preaching is not an individual act. It is a communal moment – the Word of God spoken within the *va* of a gathered people. When done with care, it becomes a sacrament of relationship.

Conclusion: The Preacher as Keeper of the *Va*

In Samoan culture, the village matai is not only a leader but a caretaker of relationships. The preacher, likewise, is a keeper of the *va*. Their task is not merely to speak truths, but to nurture the sacred spaces between hearts, between generations, and between humanity and God.

To *teu le va* in preaching is to restore trust, rebuild bridges, and rekindle belonging. It is to speak in such a way that people feel seen, known, and loved – by the church and by God.

In a time when so many youth feel dislocated – culturally, spiritually, emotionally – this is not a minor concern. It is at the heart of the gospel. For the gospel is itself an act of *teu le va* – God tending the sacred space between heaven and earth, that we might be reconciled and made whole.

Let preaching be part of that reconciling work. Let it cherish the *va*. Let it speak not over people, but with them. Let it become, once more, a source of life.

5 — Identity and Spirituality: The Heart and Lungs of Faith

The Samoan worldview is richly textured, woven together by threads of genealogy, land, spirit, and language. At the core of this worldview lies the concept of *fa'asinomaga* – identity – and *agaga* – spirit. These are not mere personal attributes; they are communal, spiritual, and embodied. They are the heart and lungs of faith. Without identity, the heart stops. Without spirit, the breath ceases. In a time when many Samoan youth in Aotearoa New Zealand feel spiritually adrift or disconnected from their church and culture, we must revisit these two vital realities and reimagine how preaching can speak to both.

This chapter explores the deep connection between *fa'asinomaga* and *agaga*, drawing particularly on the insights of Tui Atua Tupua Tamasese Ta'isi Efi. It asks how preaching – when it is attuned to cultural identity and spiritual truth – can become a life-giving act that does more than transmit doctrine. It can form identity. It can restore dignity. It can awaken a dormant spirit.

The Wisdom of Tui Atua: Identity as Sacred Memory

Tui Atua, former Head of State of Samoa and a renowned scholar and orator, has long spoken of identity as being rooted in *vā* (relational space), *gafa* (genealogy), and *talatu'u* (sacred stories and values). He reminds us that Samoan identity is not individualistic, but relational and historical. It is carried in stories, songs, rituals, and spiritual connection with both ancestors and land. One's *fa'asinomaga* is not chosen; it is received, honoured, and lived into.

In his writings, Tui Atua articulates the pain of dislocation – the sense that when we are cut off from language, land, or genealogy, we lose part of ourselves. For diaspora Samoans, especially young people born in New Zealand, this can be a source of spiritual disorientation. They are Samoan, but not fluent in the language. They are Christian, but not always connected to the church of their parents. They feel the tension between their inherited faith and their lived experience.

Tui Atua's theology is one of reclamation. It invites youth to see their identity not as fragmented, but as layered. Not as deficient, but as evolving. In this view, preaching must not reinforce guilt over cultural loss, but instead affirm the sacredness of each person's journey. It must help youth name who they are – in all their hybridity – and find God in that naming.

The Interplay of *Fa'asinomaga* and *Agaga*

Identity and spirit are inseparable. To know who you are is to know whose you are – to know your *vā* with God, your ancestors, your family, and your future. When preaching neglects identity, it risks becoming abstract or irrelevant. When it neglects spirit, it risks becoming moralistic or empty.

Agaga, the Samoan word for spirit, also means breath, wind, or life force. It is the same word used in biblical texts to describe the Spirit of God. The breath that hovered over the waters in Genesis. The Spirit that filled Jesus at baptism. The wind that rushed through Pentecost. *Agaga* is not a ghostly idea – it is the presence of life. It animates the body, the community, and the Word.

A sermon that honours *fa'asinomaga* helps listeners remember who they are. A sermon that honours *agaga* helps listeners come alive. These two movements – remembrance and awakening – are central to preaching in the CCCS today.

Naming the Crisis: Disconnection and Silence

Many young people in CCCS congregations express a feeling of being "spiritually silent." They attend church out of obligation, not encounter. They sit through sermons that feel like lectures, not living words. Some are unsure whether the God they hear about from the pulpit has any relevance to their lives.

This crisis is not simply one of faith, but of identity. When youth do not see themselves reflected in the church – in its language, leadership, or liturgy – they begin to drift. Their *fa'asinomaga* is not being affirmed. Their *agaga* is not being fed.

In this context, preaching must shift. It must become an act of spiritual restoration. It must speak in ways that awaken a sense of belonging, purpose, and presence. It must help youth hear, not just with their ears, but with their hearts: "You are seen. You are loved. You are part of God's story."

Preaching Identity: The Sacred Work of Naming

In Scripture, names matter. They are not labels, but declarations of purpose and identity. God renames Abram and Sarai, calls Moses by name from the burning bush, and speaks Jesus' name with affirmation at baptism: "You are my beloved."

Preachers today must recover the power of naming. In their sermons, they must name the realities young people live with – racism, pressure to succeed, cultural confusion, isolation, mental health struggles – and speak these aloud with compassion and hope. When the preacher names what is real, the listener feels known.

But preachers must also name the deeper identity of youth: as bearers of God's image, as descendants of a proud Samoan lineage, as loved without condition. This is not sentimentality. It is theology. Naming is a sacred act. It can shift shame into dignity, confusion into clarity, silence into voice.

This practice also aligns with the Samoan tradition of oral proclamation, in which names, titles, and lineages are remembered aloud in public ceremonies. This is not mere flattery – it is theology in action. Naming who someone is affirms their place in the community, their dignity, their belonging.

When the preacher does this faithfully, the pulpit becomes not a place of judgment, but a place of affirmation. It says, "You are part of this family. You are not invisible."

Preaching Spirit: The Sacred Work of Breathing

Preaching must also be animated by *agaga*. This means sermons must not only instruct but inspire. They must carry breath. Too often, preaching is exhausted – weighed down by moralising, too many words, or fear of being irrelevant. But when the Spirit is alive in the preacher – when they have prayed, listened, and opened themselves to God – then the sermon carries weight.

The goal is not entertainment, but encounter. A sermon should move the heart, stir the conscience, open the imagination. It should feel like fresh air to a weary soul.

This requires a shift in preparation. Preachers must not only ask, "What should I say?" but also, "What does the Spirit want to breathe into this community?" It requires trust – in God, in the text, and in the people.

Preaching animated by *agaga* is not showy or dramatic. It may be quiet. It may be simple. But it has power – because it connects. It revives. It heals.

A sermon that is truly inspired by the Spirit does not need to shout to be heard. It needs to resonate. The preacher becomes a channel, not a performer. And the Spirit works through tone, timing, silence, and metaphor – not just content.

Practices for Preaching Identity and Spirit

To preach in a way that honours both *fa'asinomaga* and *agaga*, preachers can adopt several spiritual and practical disciplines:

- **Pray in both languages** – even brief phrases in Samoan and English can help hold identity in tension and reverence.

- **Use stories** – both biblical and contemporary, especially those that reflect youth experience and Pacific culture.

- **Speak to the heart** – avoid only intellectual or moralistic tones; speak with emotional depth.

- **Include liturgical moments that name identity** – blessings, affirmations, testimonies.

- **Ask reflective questions in sermons** – to invite inner dialogue and awaken the spirit.

- **Preach with vulnerability** – share struggles, doubts, and hope; modelling authenticity reaffirms identity.

- **Draw from Samoan cultural imagery** – tapa cloths, canoes, land, ancestors, the ocean, the stars – to root sermons in cultural imagination.

- **Involve youth in sermon creation** – invite their voices into the preparation process, even anonymously, to ensure their reality is heard.

- **Let silence be part of the sermon** – moments of pause can become space for the Spirit to breathe.

- **Use visual or musical illustrations** – these speak to the imagination and can connect across cultural and generational divides.

Conclusion: A Preaching of Wholeness

When *faʻasinomaga* and *agaga* are separated, faith becomes fragmented. Youth feel they must choose between their culture and their church, their questions and their beliefs. But when preaching holds these together – naming identity and breathing spirit – faith becomes whole again.

Tui Atua reminds us that our ancestors live on in our memory, our bones, and our breath. The gospel, too, must live in our memory and breath – not just in rules, but in stories, spirit, and identity.

Let preaching in the CCCS be a preaching of wholeness. Let it be the heart and lungs of faith for a new generation – beating with identity, breathing with spirit, and alive with the presence of God.

For the preacher, this is sacred work. It is more than proclaiming the gospel – it is embodying it in such a way that the listener feels remembered, restored, and renewed. The words may be ordinary. The structure may be simple. But when spoken with truth and breath and love, a sermon can become an act of healing.

Preaching, then, becomes a gift. Not a burden. Not a performance. But a gift – to the people, to God, and to the preacher themselves. For in giving voice to identity and allowing the Spirit to breathe, the preacher, too, is renewed. This is what it means to speak life. This is what it means to preach the gospel in a Samoan key.

6 — *Toe Timata le Ūpega*: A Samoan Framework for Change

The Samoan proverb *"Toe timata le ūpega"* – "Let us return and repair the net" – carries within it a rich cultural and spiritual metaphor. On the surface, it refers to the simple task of mending a fishing net that has frayed or torn. But at a deeper level, it symbolises the restoration of relationships, the revitalisation of communal life, and the renewal of purpose. It suggests that the damage sustained over time – whether in relationships, faith, or culture – is not the end of the story. We can begin again. We can restore what has been lost. We can weave a stronger, more resilient net.

In this chapter, we explore how *toe timata le ūpega* can provide a framework for change within the Congregational Christian Church Samoa (CCCS), especially in its Aotearoa New Zealand context. This metaphor speaks into the heart of our challenge: how do we address the disconnection between generations, the disillusionment of youth, and the perceived irrelevance of preaching? Rather than abandoning the net or continuing to cast it in futility, this chapter calls us to mend it – with courage, humility, and hope.

The Net as a Living Symbol

Fishing has long been a central practice in Samoan life – not just for sustenance, but as a cultural rhythm and spiritual metaphor. The *ūpega* (net) represents community: interconnected, purposeful, woven strand by strand. When a net breaks, it is not discarded – it is examined, cleaned, and mended. This practical wisdom becomes a powerful image for church life.

In a congregational setting, the *ūpega* can be seen as the web of relationships, rituals, language, and theological practices that hold a church together. When young people drift away, when sermons go unheard, when elders feel frustrated and unheard, the net is showing signs of wear. But that does not mean it has lost its value. It means it needs our attention.

Toe timata le ūpega means we stop, we reflect, and we begin again – not from scratch, but from the wisdom of what has already been. This proverb becomes a call to spiritual discernment, to communal repair, and to a brave reimagination of what church could become.

Signs the Net is Tearing: Voices from the Community

In the research interviews that underpin this book, several recurring themes emerged from youth and young adults in the CCCS. These voices reveal where the net is fraying:

- "I go to church, but I don't feel like it's for me."

- "The language is too hard. I zone out."

- "It's always the same message – obey, be humble, serve. But I want to know what God has to do with my life now."

- "We're not against the church. We just don't know how to belong in it anymore."

These are not statements of rebellion. They are laments. They are expressions of longing – for relevance, connection, authenticity, and meaning. They point to a gap between the experience of the older generation (who often find deep value in traditional preaching, language, and ritual) and the spiritual hunger of the younger generation (who seek faith that speaks into their lived reality in Aotearoa).

The *ūpega* is under strain – pulled between cultures, languages, and expectations. Some holes in the net are the result of generational misunderstanding. Others stem from rigid leadership models or an unwillingness to change. Still others come from shame and silence – especially around topics like mental health, sexuality, or failure, which are rarely addressed from the pulpit.

But to name the tear is the first act of healing. When we see the gap, we are invited to step into it – not to close it prematurely, but to understand it, hold it, and mend it with care.

The Theology of Starting Again

Practical and Theological Meanings

According to the accounts of the call of the disciples in Matthew and Mark Jesus selected his very first disciples from local fishermen at the sea of Galilee. Matthew (4:18-22) states that: "As [Jesus] walked by the Sea of Galilee, he saw two brothers, Simon, who is called Peter, and Andrew his brother, casting a net into the sea – for they were fishers. And he said to them, 'Follow me, and I will make you fishers of people.'"

Similarly, Mark (1:16-17) explains that "As Jesus passed along the Sea of Galilee, he saw Simon and his brother Andrew casting a net into the sea, for they were fishermen. And Jesus said to them, 'Follow me and I will make you fish for people.'"

Each day they mended, prepared, and repaired their nets, ready for the next catch. Fishing was their daily work, providing food and income for their families and community. Jesus first called Peter and Andrew while they were casting their nets in the Sea of Galilee. The link between preaching the gospel and the work of a fisherman is clear in both Matthew's and Mark's stories.

John's Gospel (21:4-8) tells of Jesus appearing to his disciples at the Sea of Tiberias after they had caught nothing all night. John makes it clear that without Jesus, their efforts would fail. Jesus saw their frustration after a night of empty nets. This story reminds us that preaching the gospel also depends on the Spirit's authority and guidance, so that sermons truly connect with and speak to their listeners.

When preaching, ministers who rely on the Spirit of Christ for guidance will be able to reach and inspire more people through their ministry. Just as a fisherman must mend his nets to catch many fish, preachers must carefully prepare their sermons to touch many hearts. In this sense, the act of repairing the net becomes a symbol for the preacher's task. The minister's responsibility is to craft and deliver the message of the gospel in a way that nourishes people's faith and helps them grow spiritually.

The preacher's main task is to stay focused on the key message, purpose, and outcome of each sermon. Every week, in the days leading up to Sunday, the minister must 're-mend' or 'repair' the fishing net – that is, their sermon. This means carefully reviewing, reflecting on, and honestly assessing their own preaching. The message must always be inclusive, effective, and connected to people's real-life experiences and struggles. The action of *toe timata/matimati* is an ongoing process – making sure the sermon remains clear in its message, relevant in its meaning, and appropriate for the congregation. The minister's ongoing work of re-evaluating and deepening their biblical and theological understanding is essential to this calling.

Ministers must take seriously the real-life situations and contexts that today's Christians face. This careful and committed approach to preaching can be understood through Hans-Georg Gadamer's idea of the "fusion of horizons." Gadamer taught that to truly understand a text, there must be a meeting between two horizons – the world of the interpreter and the world of the text itself. This fusion of horizons is part of what he called the hermeneutic circle – an ongoing, open conversation between the interpreter and the text. It also reflects the I–Thou relationship, where genuine understanding requires deep openness to the experience of the other and respect for perspectives that go beyond one's own.

Gadamer's idea of the fusion of horizons has two parts – it brings together the world of the interpreter and the world of the text in both preparing and delivering a sermon. This approach helps the minister or preacher connect the cultural, economic, social, political, and religious background of the biblical text with their own understanding of today's world. Through this process, a clear framework is formed for shaping the sermon, ensuring that the message of the chosen passage is meaningful and relevant to the congregation. In short, when the preacher understands both the world of the Bible and the world of the listeners, the sermon can speak powerfully to people's real lives.

In Scripture, we see countless examples of God inviting people to start again:

- Noah and his family step into a new world after the flood.

- The Israelites are called to return from exile and rebuild.

- Jesus calls discouraged disciples to cast their nets again (John 21).

- The early church learns to reimagine its identity through the inclusion of Gentiles.

The biblical narrative does not shy away from failure, rupture, or disappointment. It shows us that beginnings are often preceded by endings – and that God is present in the in-between. *Toe timata le ūpega* is not only a cultural proverb, but a theological invitation. It echoes God's faithfulness in the face of human limitation. It invites us to be co-weavers of a new future.

This theology gives courage to communities that feel tired or stuck. It gives permission to rethink preaching styles, to create new spaces for youth expression, to question the usefulness of inherited practices, and to honour the Spirit's movement in fresh ways.

Case Study: The Youth-Led Service in Māngere

One congregation in South Auckland experimented with handing over a full Sunday morning service to its youth group – from planning to preaching. The leadership team offered support, but not control. The youth chose the songs, wrote the prayers, dramatised the Scripture reading, and shared testimonies instead of a traditional sermon.

The result was electric. Elders were moved to tears. Some confessed it was the first time they had truly "heard" the gospel from their grandchildren. Young people stayed after church, talking with older members. The *vā* was renewed.

The following week, the preaching elder acknowledged the risk that had been taken. "But it reminded us," he said, "that the Spirit speaks through many voices. And our job is not to control the net – but to mend it, extend it, and trust that it will hold."

This is *toe timata le ūpega* in action: a community stepping out of routine to rediscover relationship.

A Framework for Reweaving the Net

If we take this proverb seriously, what practical changes might it lead to in our churches?

1. **Hold Listening Forums** – Create regular, intergenerational spaces where youth and elders can speak and listen without judgment.

2. **Mentor, Don't Just Preach** – Encourage leaders to walk alongside youth, not just speak to them from the pulpit. Vaitusi Nofoaiga, writing from a Samoan perspective on discipleship in the Gospel of Matthew, explains that following Jesus can be understood through the Samoan term *tautuaileva* – service carried out "in-between spaces." *Tautuaileva*, according to Nofoaiga, describes the role of ministers or *faifeau* as humble servants who care for the physical, emotional, and spiritual well-being of God's people. In Samoan thought, a *faifeau* or disciple is a *tautua* – a servant – not a leader or someone who holds authority over others. The main calling of a *tautua* as a disciple is to serve others, not to dominate or control them.

3. **Diversify the Pulpit** – Invite young adults, women, and laypeople to preach occasionally or share testimonies.

4. **Teach the Language with Grace** – Offer Samoan language learning in the church context that is not tied to shame or failure.

These concerns of the youth are clearly expressed by Jemaima Tiatia in her book *Caught Between Cultures*:

"The youth voice has been suppressed to such an extent that Island born church members subjugate, ignore, and belittle the significance of the ideas and values that the New Zealand born wish to implement in order to cater for own their needs. The Island born elders need to acknowledge that their youth are living in a contemporary society, a completely different context from which they themselves were brought up. The church should therefore adapt accordingly."

The communal way of life once centred on harmony and peace – planted to nurture the relationship between culture and the gospel – has been replaced by a misunderstanding of *pule*, now seen as leading through power and control. The dominant attitudes of some *matai* in exercising their *pule* have created a strong sense of oppression among parish members, especially the youth. Tiatia notes that:

> "A perceived lack of consciousness of disadvantage or oppression can be partially explained by the historical and cultural ideologies of [Samoan] community which relies on family solidarity and a traditionally hierarchical social structure."

5. **Preach Contextually** – Encourage sermons that speak to the current issues facing young people: racism, climate change, sexuality, purpose.

6. **Create Parallel Worship Spaces** – Consider youth services that allow different formats and expressions while still being connected to the wider church.

7. **Celebrate Mistakes as Learning** – When things don't go to plan, model grace, not blame.

These are not revolutionary changes – but they are intentional acts of mending. Each is a knot tied back into the net, each a gesture of trust that the next generation is not lost, but waiting.

Courage and Creativity: The Twin Threads

To return and repair the net requires two qualities often overlooked in institutional settings: courage and creativity.

Courage is needed to name what isn't working, to risk failure, to let go of control. Creativity is needed to imagine new forms of faithfulness, to experiment with language, music, and message, and to trust that God is not bound by our traditions.

Our elders had courage – in crossing oceans, in planting churches, in keeping faith alive through hardship. Now we are called to that same courage – not in preservation, but in transformation.

And we must remember that creativity is not a threat to faith. It is part of it. God creates. Jesus tells stories. The Spirit moves unpredictably. To preach creatively, to organise differently, to listen in new ways – these are not distractions. They are signs that the net is being reformed for new waters.

Conclusion: Weaving a Future Together

Toe timata le ūpega is more than a metaphor. It is a call to action. It invites us to see preaching not as a static tradition, but as a living practice – one that must be tended, renewed, and shared.

In a time of change and challenge, this proverb offers hope. It says: we are not finished. We can begin again. The net can hold. But only if we are willing to sit together, listen deeply, and mend the strands that connect us.

Let this be the work of every preacher, elder, and young person: to honour the old threads, to tie new ones, and to cast again – with faith that the next catch will come not through control, but through connection. Through a net repaired by love.

Let us return. Let us begin again. Let us mend the net – together.

7 — Preaching That Connects: Language, Imagery, and Context

Preaching is more than just a spoken message delivered from a pulpit. It is a sacred encounter – a weaving of Word and world, a bridge between God's story and the stories of the people. In the Congregational Christian Church Samoa (CCCS), preaching holds immense cultural and spiritual weight. It is the heart of Sunday worship, the moment when silence gives way to proclamation, and when faith is voiced aloud for the community to receive.

Yet, as many of our youth have expressed, there is a growing disconnection between the pulpit and the pew – especially for younger generations raised in Aotearoa New Zealand. Many sermons fail to speak into their reality. The traditional forms of Samoan oratory, while beautiful and rich, can feel distant, repetitive, or inaccessible to those who do not share the same linguistic fluency or cultural reference points.

This chapter is a call to preachers in the CCCS – both ordained and lay – to reflect on how language, imagery, and context can make or break the effectiveness of a sermon. It offers practical guidance for crafting sermons that honour our cultural heritage while also making space for relevance, clarity, and connection.

Why Language Matters

Language is never neutral. It shapes not only what we say, but how we are heard. In CCCS churches across New Zealand, the primary language of preaching remains Samoan. For older members of the congregation, this is comforting and affirming. It is the language of their faith, their prayers, and their memories.

However, for many youth and young adults – even those who understand spoken Samoan – the deeper theological language, idioms, and formal structures of preaching can feel alienating. Some understand the words but not the meaning. Others understand neither. The result is that they sit in church out of respect, but disconnect internally.

Effective preaching does not require abandoning the Samoan language. Instead, it calls for creative bilingualism. A sermon can be primarily in Samoan, but interwoven with English to illuminate key ideas. Alternatively, a preacher might summarise in English after delivering a complex theological point in Samoan. This honours both generations – those for whom Samoan is sacred, and those for whom English is a necessary access point.

Bilingual Preaching: Principles for Practice

- **Signpost Transitions Clearly:** When switching languages, let the congregation know. For example, *"O lea ua ou faamatala i le gagana Peretania* – let me now explain this part in English."

- **Translate Key Phrases, Not Everything:** Avoid word-for-word translation. Instead, focus on conveying the core message in both languages.

- **Use Parallel Repetition:** Say a meaningful phrase in Samoan, then echo it in English with similar rhythm. This reinforces the message.

- **Avoid Code-Switching Just for Effect:** Changing languages should serve clarity, not confuse.

- **Reflect Your Audience:** In youth services or intergenerational gatherings, err on the side of accessibility. Let the language serve the listener, not the other way around.

Imagery That Speaks to Both Worlds

Traditional Samoan preaching often draws on agricultural, familial, and communal metaphors – the plantation, the chiefly house, the extended family. These images carry deep cultural resonance for many, but can feel distant to youth who have grown up in urban New Zealand.

This does not mean we discard traditional imagery. Rather, we expand our palette. A sermon can draw on the *fale*, but also on the classroom. It can reference the *ava* ceremony and the rugby team. It can move between biblical parables and social media culture.

Youth are highly visual. They respond to story, metaphor, and vivid language. Abstract theological concepts can become accessible when grounded in images they understand.

Practical Imagery Tips

- **Anchor Theology in Everyday Life**: Talk about God's grace using the metaphor of a second chance in a school exam. Describe the church as a team where every role matters.

- **Use Technology and Pop Culture Thoughtfully**: Reference movies, music, or current events, but only to deepen the message – not to appear "cool."

- **Revisit Samoan Metaphors with Fresh Eyes**: Explain the significance of the *siapo*, or the making of a mat, in ways that highlight spiritual meaning.

- **Tell Stories**: Personal anecdotes, especially those that show vulnerability or struggle, build connection.

Themes That Matter

One of the main critiques from youth is that preaching often repeats a narrow set of themes – obedience, humility, service – without connecting them to real-life issues. These are essential Christian values, but they must be grounded in relevance.

Youth today are navigating complex realities: racism, climate change, mental health, cultural identity, family pressure, social media, sexuality, peer pressure, and questions about God's relevance. They are not looking for shallow answers – but they are hungry for sermons that acknowledge their lived experience.

How to Choose Relevant Themes

- **Listen First**: Attend youth gatherings. Ask questions. Find out what issues are keeping young people up at night.

- **Preach to the Margins**: Consider those who feel like outsiders in the church. Preaching should always make space for the unheard.

- **Link Scripture to Struggle**: Don't just retell the Bible story. Ask – what does this mean for a teenager feeling anxious, or a university student questioning their faith?

- **Include Ethical and Social Dimensions**: Faith is not just personal; it is communal and political. Preach justice, compassion, and responsibility.

The Balance of Oratory and Accessibility

Samoan preaching is traditionally structured and formal, shaped by oratorical rhythm and rhetorical techniques. There is dignity in this approach – it affirms the status of the preacher and the sacredness of the Word. But if this style is delivered with too much distance or rigidity, it can create barriers.

The challenge is not to abandon Samoan oratory, but to adapt it. Accessibility does not mean lowering the standard – it means widening the reach.

Adapting Oratory for Connection

- **Vary Your Voice**: Use changes in tone, pace, and volume to hold attention.

- **Engage the Audience**: Ask rhetorical questions. Make space for laughter. Include moments of silence for reflection.

- **Use a Clear Structure**: Have a beginning, middle, and end. Let your points build.

- **Avoid Overuse of Formal Language**: Speak naturally. The pulpit is not a place for performance, but for presence.

The Power of Visual Aids and Storytelling

In a media-saturated world, young people are used to receiving information through images, stories, and digital media. Incorporating simple visuals or props into preaching – even just holding an item or showing a photo – can awaken curiosity and deepen understanding.

Storytelling, especially when it is honest and personal, is one of the most effective tools a preacher has. Jesus taught in parables for a reason. A story allows the listener to find themselves within the message.

Ways to Incorporate Story and Symbol

- **Begin with a Visual Metaphor**: e.g. hold up a cracked phone screen when talking about brokenness.

- **Tell Stories from Your Own Life**: Not to glorify yourself, but to show your humanity.

- **Use Intergenerational Testimonies**: Ask both youth and elders to share how faith impacts them.

- **Include Biblical Reenactments or Drama**: Involve the congregation in creatively engaging the text.

Preaching as Dialogue, Not Monologue

One of the most transformative shifts in preaching is to understand it not as a one-way delivery, but as a conversation. Of course, the preacher is the one speaking – but good preaching listens before it speaks, and invites ongoing reflection afterward.

This can be done in various ways:

- Invite feedback after the service.

- Pose open-ended questions during the sermon.

- Offer space for people to respond with their own stories.

- Preach in series, allowing a theme to develop over time.

Dialogue does not undermine authority. It deepens it. It says to the congregation: "You matter. Your questions matter. God is already at work in your life."

Conclusion: Faithful and Fresh

To preach well in the CCCS context today is to walk a fine line – between tradition and innovation, reverence and relevance, the sacred language of our ancestors and the everyday language of our youth. It is not an easy task. But it is a vital one.

We do not preach to impress. We preach to connect. We preach to heal. We preach to bring the Word to life in the hearts of those who are listening – whether they are 18 or 80.

Let every sermon be an act of bridge-building. Let every preacher be a student of the people, as well as the Bible. Let every pulpit become a place where stories meet Scripture, where culture meets calling, where the Spirit speaks in many tongues.

For this generation, and the next. For God's glory, and the people's good.

Let us preach. Let us connect. Let us begin again – with courage, humility, and hope.

8 — Beyond the Pulpit: Youth Participation in Worship

Worship is the heart of congregational life. It is where the people of God gather to offer praise, receive teaching, and be reminded of their identity as the body of Christ. In the Congregational Christian Church Samoa (CCCS), worship has traditionally followed a formal and structured pattern. It is deeply rooted in the Samoan cultural ethos of respect, *faaaloalo*, honour for tradition, and reverence for God. While these foundations remain vital, the reality facing many congregations in Aotearoa New Zealand is that young people often feel like observers rather than participants.

This chapter explores how churches can move "beyond the pulpit" by actively involving youth in leading, shaping, and embodying worship. It offers practical suggestions and cultural reflections on how music, testimony, drama, and digital media can revive engagement. More importantly, it considers how participation in worship helps young people build spiritual confidence and find their voice within the faith community.

Why Participation Matters

The structure of CCCS worship has traditionally placed the pulpit and preacher at the centre. This model, while honouring the authority of Scripture and preaching, can unintentionally marginalise the contributions of others – especially youth. Many young people grow up attending church services faithfully, yet reach adolescence with no meaningful sense of ownership over what happens in worship.

Research interviews revealed a shared sentiment among youth: "We are at church, but church is not in us." They attend out of respect for parents or grandparents, but often feel like their presence makes little difference. They do not see themselves reflected in the language, music, or stories that dominate the service. And rarely are they asked to contribute.

This lack of engagement is not a reflection of youth disinterest in God or spirituality. On the contrary, many are deeply curious about faith, justice, and meaning. But when worship feels inaccessible or irrelevant, they disengage – not because they don't care, but because they don't feel invited to matter.

Participation matters because it shifts worship from something we watch to something we do. It creates space for gifts to emerge. It affirms that every member of the body – regardless of age – has something to offer. And it helps young people see that worship is not just a duty to perform, but a relationship to enter.

Pathways to Youth Participation

1. Involve Youth in Worship Planning

True participation begins not with performance but with preparation. Involving youth in planning worship gives them a sense of ownership and agency. This can begin with small steps: inviting a group of young people to meet with the preacher to discuss the Bible reading for the week, to suggest a theme, or to brainstorm how the service might reflect the issues young people are facing.

For example, one church in Wellington began a monthly "intergenerational planning team" where youth and elders worked together to design creative services. The result was greater understanding across generations – and services that included more relevant language, visuals, and stories.

When youth are part of the planning, they are more likely to feel invested in the outcome. And when they feel invested, they bring their creativity, passion, and energy to the space.

2. Music and Song

Music is often the most immediate way young people connect with worship. Many grew up singing traditional CCCS hymns in Samoan, but also listen daily to contemporary Christian music, gospel, hip-hop, and other genres.

Rather than framing these styles as competing, churches can explore ways to blend traditional and contemporary music. Some congregations now include one youth-led song during the offering or communion. Others have formed youth bands or vocal groups that lead worship in English and Samoan.

It is important that musical participation is not seen as entertainment, but as ministry. Young people should be mentored in the theology of worship, the spiritual discipline of leading music, and the purpose of song in shaping the hearts of the congregation.

3. Testimonies and Spoken Word

One of the most powerful ways youth can participate is by sharing their own faith stories. Testimonies do not require perfect theology or eloquence – they require honesty. And when youth speak from the heart about their journey with God, their struggles and hopes, the entire congregation is enriched.

Some churches have introduced "Faith Moments" as part of the service, where a young person shares a short reflection on how their faith connects with their life – school, family, friendships, social justice, or cultural identity.

Others have encouraged the use of spoken word poetry – a form of creative expression that allows young people to explore biblical themes through rhythm and performance. When done well, this form of participation bridges the gap between ancient text and contemporary life.

4. Drama and Storytelling

Dramatising Scripture readings, acting out parables, or performing short skits can bring energy and insight to familiar stories. Drama engages not only the mind but the body and imagination. It helps young people move from abstract ideas to lived experience.

A youth group in Hamilton, for example, reimagined the parable of the Good Samaritan in a school setting – with a bullied student left ignored by peers, until a "Samaritan" stepped in. The performance opened up conversations about compassion, exclusion, and courage.

When youth see themselves as storytellers of the gospel – not just receivers – they begin to understand preaching and proclamation as something they too can embody.

5. Digital Media and Visual Arts

Today's young people are digital natives. They communicate through images, videos, memes, and social media. The church can harness this familiarity by incorporating visual elements into worship – projected images during Scripture readings, short video reflections, or youth-created multimedia prayers.

One Pacific youth group created a short film exploring the theme of forgiveness, which was shown as the "sermon" for a Sunday service. It sparked deep conversations and gave young people a sense of accomplishment.

Visual participation also includes creating worship banners, painting, photography, or even using TikTok-style reels to summarise the Sunday message. These forms of participation are not distractions from worship – they are expressions of it, translated through a new lens.

Building Spiritual Confidence and Voice

Involving youth in worship is not just about filling service slots. It is about forming disciples. It is about helping young people discover that their voice matters in the community of faith.

Participation builds confidence. It teaches skills of leadership, communication, teamwork, and theological reflection. It helps youth move from passive attendance to active ministry. But this does not happen automatically. It requires mentorship.

Elders and ministers must walk alongside youth – not just to instruct, but to encourage. This means affirming their efforts, helping them prepare, offering constructive feedback, and being willing to step aside so that others can step up.

Balancing Tradition and Innovation

Some worry that involving youth will lead to a loss of reverence or the dilution of tradition. But the goal is not to replace tradition – it is to renew it. Samoan culture itself is dynamic and adaptive. The early missionaries translated the gospel into cultural forms; now it is time for a new generation to do the same.

We can maintain the dignity of CCCS worship while making space for diverse expressions. We can uphold the authority of Scripture while allowing young people to interpret it through their own lens. We can sing the old hymns and introduce new songs. We can keep preaching in the pulpit – and hear God's voice from the floor, the pew, the guitar, the video screen.

The balance is found not in compromise, but in collaboration. When elders and youth co-create worship, both are transformed.

Overcoming Barriers

Of course, there are challenges. Some congregations may resist change. Some elders may feel unsure about how to mentor youth. Some young people may fear failure or judgement. To overcome these barriers, churches must:

- Create a culture of experimentation and grace.

- Celebrate small successes.

- Provide training and support.

- Emphasise that participation is not about performance but presence.

Conclusion: A Worshipping Church, Together

A worshipping church is not one where a few speak and many listen – it is one where all are drawn into the mystery of God together. When youth participate, worship becomes more than a routine. It becomes a conversation. A discovery. A celebration.

To move beyond the pulpit is not to abandon it. It is to surround it with stories, songs, images, and voices that together proclaim the love of God. When young people find their place in this proclamation, they are not just future leaders – they are church now.

Let us be brave enough to open the doors, humble enough to learn, and faithful enough to trust that God is still speaking – through every generation.

Let us worship together. Let us lead together. Let us grow in faith – together.

9 — Bridging the Gap: Tools for Ministers and Lay Leaders

In every generation, the church is called to discern how best to proclaim the timeless gospel in a changing world. Ministers and lay leaders within the Congregational Christian Church Samoa (CCCS) face this challenge acutely in the Aotearoa New Zealand context. Here, young people grow up negotiating two cultures – Samoan and Kiwi – and often feel disconnected from a church that seems to speak primarily to their elders. The result is a growing gap: between pulpit and pew, tradition and innovation, older and younger generations.

This chapter offers practical tools to help bridge that gap. It provides strategies for reshaping preaching and worship to better engage youth, guidance on running youth-focused service series, and ways to build intergenerational trust and dialogue. Above all, it encourages ministers and lay leaders to see themselves as facilitators of transformation – people who model courage, creativity, and openness to God's ongoing work.

1. Reframing the Role of Preacher and Leader

In the CCCS tradition, the preacher holds significant authority. This is a gift – but it can also be a barrier if leadership is understood only in terms of control rather than collaboration. To engage youth effectively, ministers must shift from being the sole voice to becoming enablers of many voices.

This does not mean giving up theological depth or pastoral oversight. Rather, it means modelling a relational style of leadership rooted in *va* – the sacred space between people. When leaders honour this relational space, they empower others to participate and grow.

Start by asking: Who else could help tell this story? What perspectives might illuminate the text differently? How can I open space for others to contribute?

2. Reshaping Preaching for Engagement

The heart of the CCCS remains its preaching. But the form and delivery of preaching must evolve to connect with younger listeners. Here are practical shifts to consider:

- **Use contemporary illustrations**: Connect Scripture with youth-relevant themes – identity, anxiety, relationships, racism, vocation, and purpose. Draw on everyday experiences, media, school life, or current events.

- **Ask questions**: Move from lecture-style sermons to interactive preaching. Pose real questions and invite reflection. Some congregations provide reflection cards or allow moments of silence to consider key ideas.

- **Use visuals or short clips**: Consider integrating images or short videos that underline the sermon theme. A picture of a tangled fishing net, a 30-second clip from a youth-created video, or a contemporary image of grace or injustice can all make Scripture come alive.

- **Vary language**: Use both English and Samoan as appropriate. Explain theological terms. Speak in ways that young people can relate to emotionally and intellectually.

3. Running a Youth-Focused Worship Series

One effective strategy is to run a special series of youth-focused services. These can be monthly, seasonal, or even a designated Youth Month. Here's how to design such a series:

- **Theme selection**: Choose themes that matter to youth. Some examples include: "Belonging", "Finding My Voice", "Hope in Hard Times", "Who Is Jesus for Me Today?", "Standing Up for Justice."

- **Collaborative planning**: Form a youth-adult planning team. Include representatives from different age groups. Encourage mutual respect. Listen more than you speak.

- **Flexible format**: Allow for creative formats – testimonies, videos, open mic responses, or drama. Don't be afraid to step outside the traditional order of service for special occasions.

- **Multi-sensory elements**: Use music, images, lighting, and movement to help worship appeal to the heart as well as the mind. Youth are more likely to engage when worship engages the whole self.

- **Celebrate participation**: Make it known that this is a space where youth are not being tested, but trusted. Let them see that their voices are heard, their creativity valued, and their spiritual insights taken seriously.

4. Training and Mentoring Young Leaders

Leadership is not a gift bestowed at adulthood – it is a calling that must be nurtured early. Ministers and elders have a vital role in mentoring emerging leaders. This requires patience, encouragement, and a long-term perspective.

Start small. Ask a young person to help read Scripture, lead a prayer, or assist with tech. Then, walk with them. Debrief afterward. Affirm their strengths. Offer gentle guidance. In time, they may lead entire services, preach short messages, or become peer mentors themselves.

Some churches have developed youth internship programs, shadowing roles, or monthly youth-led services to support this process. Others rotate leadership roles in youth groups so everyone has a turn at planning, leading, and reflecting.

A culture of mentorship fosters spiritual growth, ownership, and confidence. It teaches that leadership is not about being the best speaker – but about serving others with integrity.

5. Intergenerational Conversation as a Spiritual Practice

The gap between generations in CCCS congregations is not only cultural or linguistic – it is often spiritual. Youth and elders interpret faith differently. This can lead to misunderstandings, disappointment, or even silent withdrawal.

One of the most powerful tools for bridging this divide is intentional conversation. Create space for stories to be shared across generations:

- **Story circles**: Invite elders to share how they came to faith, what church meant in their youth, and what their hopes are for the next generation. Then invite youth to share their experiences, dreams, and challenges.

- **Faith interviews**: Pair youth and elders to interview each other about spiritual questions. What does prayer mean to you? What do you fear? Where have you seen God lately?

- **Dialogue services**: Build services that include intergenerational preaching teams, where a youth and elder share reflections side by side.

These practices can build empathy, dismantle stereotypes, and deepen relationships. They transform the church from a place of passive transmission to one of mutual discovery.

6. Tools for Digital Engagement

In a digital world, ministers and lay leaders must also consider how to engage youth online. This does not mean replicating TikTok trends, but it does mean understanding the platforms youth inhabit.

- **Short weekly reflections**: Consider posting a 2-minute video message each week from the preacher summarising the sermon or offering a thought for the week.

- **Youth social media teams**: Empower tech-savvy young people to help run the church's online presence, share announcements, or post encouraging Scripture.

- **Livestreaming**: Make worship more accessible for youth who cannot always attend physically – due to sport, work, or other commitments. Include youth in running the tech.

- **Group chats and devotionals**: Set up messaging groups where Scripture and prayer prompts are shared throughout the week.

When used wisely, digital tools can extend the reach of pastoral care, deepen faith, and create meaningful spiritual connections.

7. Holding Courage and Compassion Together

Change is not easy. It takes courage to try new things, to invite youth into sacred spaces, to preach differently, or to lead with less control. But it also takes compassion – for elders who fear losing tradition, for youth still finding their voice, and for ministers navigating competing expectations.

Bridging the gap means holding both. Courage without compassion can alienate. Compassion without courage can stagnate. But when leaders commit to walking the middle way, they model the love and wisdom of Christ.

8. Sustaining the Journey

Transformation is not a one-off event – it is a lifelong journey. Ministers and lay leaders must commit to ongoing growth, evaluation, and learning. Some ways to sustain the journey include:

- **Peer support**: Form minister clusters or lay leader groups who meet monthly to share ideas, pray, and reflect on challenges.

- **Training workshops**: Attend or host learning days focused on youth engagement, preaching renewal, or cultural identity in ministry.

- **Youth feedback**: Regularly seek input from young people. What's working? What's not? What are they hungry for?

- **Celebrate change**: Mark milestones. Celebrate the first youth-led prayer, the first drama, the first bilingual sermon. Let the congregation see that change is not loss – it is life.

Conclusion: Becoming a Church That Bridges

Bridging the gap is not about pleasing everyone all the time. It is about creating a church where everyone belongs. A church where Samoan identity is celebrated and transformed through the Spirit. A church where young people know they matter. A church where tradition and innovation kiss.

Ministers and lay leaders have the tools to begin this work. It starts with a willingness to listen. A commitment to empower. A faith that believes the Spirit still speaks.

To bridge the gap is to follow Christ – the one who crossed from heaven to earth, from word to flesh, from the eternal to the everyday. When we do likewise, we become bearers of grace in a divided world.

And the net begins to be mended.

And the people begin to return.

And the gospel is preached anew – in every voice, every generation, every tongue.

10 — The Future Is Now: Reimagining the Church We Love

The Congregational Christian Church Samoa (CCCS) stands at a crossroad. In New Zealand and across the Pacific diaspora, the question confronting us is no longer whether change is needed – but how, and how urgently, we are prepared to respond. Youth are drifting away from the pews. Worship feels distant to many who have grown up in a new world of digital media, hybrid identities, and bicultural tension. Yet amid this challenge, there is also a deep wellspring of hope: the potential for a renewed church that is both rooted and responsive, honouring the past while speaking with courage into the future.

This chapter issues a call – not just for cautious reform, but for creative reimagination. What kind of church might we become if we listened closely to the voice of the Spirit already stirring among our young people? How might preaching, worship, and leadership evolve to reflect the vibrant, bicultural lives of CCCS youth? What decisions must we make now to ensure the church we love does not become a museum of memory, but a living movement of mission?

1. Urgency Without Panic

Urgency is not the same as anxiety. While many CCCS leaders are aware of declining youth engagement, there is often a tendency to either downplay the problem or respond with fear-based reaction. Neither is helpful.

Instead, urgency can be a form of spiritual attentiveness – a willingness to see clearly, speak honestly, and act boldly. The church must resist the temptation to frame youth disengagement as mere disobedience or disrespect. It is often grief in disguise. Many young people do not leave because they no longer believe in God. They leave because they no longer believe the church speaks to their world.

The task is not to chase relevance in superficial ways, but to rediscover the gospel's relevance for this generation. This takes time, humility, and the courage to experiment.

2. Honouring Tradition While Innovating

Reimagining the church does not mean discarding everything that has gone before. Our task is not to tear down the *fale*, but to open its windows and invite in fresh air. Samoan oratory, sacred music, and liturgical rhythm have power. But like all living traditions, they must be reinterpreted for each new generation.

Innovation does not mean abandoning depth. It means asking:

- How can these treasures of our faith be translated afresh into the lives of young people?

- Can the metaphors of Jesus be sung in both Samoan and English?

- Can the pulse of *fa'asamoa* find new rhythm in a New Zealand landscape?

- Can we preach with the fire of old while using the language and imagery of today?

The answer must be yes – because to fail in this work is to risk losing the very people we seek to serve.

3. Imagining the CCCS in 20 Years

Let us imagine two futures.

In one future, CCCS services continue largely unchanged. Preaching remains formal and abstract. Youth are present for duty but not for joy. English is limited to announcements. Music reflects only elder preferences. Slowly, the church becomes a place of nostalgia rather than nurture. Numbers decline. Leadership ages. Buildings are full of echoes.

In another future, the CCCS embraces courageous change. Youth are mentored and trained to lead. Bilingual services become the norm. Sermons are preached with both theological depth and cultural awareness. Services feature testimony, music, and media crafted by young people. Dialogue replaces monologue. Faith is alive, embodied, and connected to real life.

In that second future, the CCCS does not simply survive. It flourishes. It becomes known not only as a guardian of tradition but as a crucible for transformation. That future is within reach – but only if the work begins now.

4. Encouraging Innovation Within the CCCS Tradition

How do we create space for innovation within a tradition that values order, reverence, and continuity? The key is spiritual imagination. We need leaders who can see beyond the structures we've inherited to the Spirit that gave them birth.

Some practical ideas include:

- **Youth Worship Labs**: Regular gatherings where young people can co-create services using traditional and new elements.

- **Bilingual Preaching Workshops**: Training ministers and lay preachers to fluently move between English and Samoan, and to craft sermons that speak across generations.

- **Cultural Exchange Services**: Host services where elders and youth exchange preaching, prayer, and music in collaborative dialogue.

- **Interdisciplinary Teams**: Form worship planning groups that include artists, theologians, youth leaders, and musicians to reflect a diversity of gifts.

- **Digital Ministry Projects**: Encourage youth to create devotional content, testimonies, or online worship experiences that reflect their faith.

Each of these initiatives requires leadership that trusts the Spirit in others. That lets go of control in order to make space. That is willing to be surprised by the new ways God might speak.

5. Lifting Up the Prophetic Voice of Youth

Youth are not simply recipients of ministry. They are prophets in their own right – often able to name injustice, hypocrisy, and irrelevance with clarity that adults avoid. Too often, we label this honesty as rebellion. But the Bible teaches us that God regularly uses young voices to proclaim truth.

The CCCS needs to create platforms where youth can speak truthfully about their spiritual hunger, their experiences of racism, their desire for a living relationship with God, and their frustration with performances of faith that lack integrity.

Let them preach. Let them write. Let them question. And most importantly, let their questions change us.

6. Reimagining the Preaching Ministry

Preaching has always been central to the CCCS identity. But in an era of multiple platforms, short attention spans, and dialogue-based learning, the traditional model of preaching must adapt.

This does not mean lowering the bar. It means learning new forms:

- **Dialogue-based Preaching**: Involve the congregation in short response times, either verbally or in writing.

- **Series-based Preaching**: Preach in 3-4 week arcs with a consistent theme – allowing time for depth and application.

- **Media-Rich Preaching**: Use music, art, or digital storytelling alongside spoken word.

- **Collaborative Preaching**: Co-preach with a youth leader or elder to model intergenerational partnership.

These innovations honour the pulpit while expanding its reach. They signal that preaching is not a monologue from the past, but a conversation for the future.

7. Building Structures That Sustain Change

For the CCCS to thrive, we must move beyond occasional youth Sundays or token gestures. We need systemic change:

- **Youth Councils with Voice and Vote**: Empower youth to shape decision-making at local and national levels.

- **Leadership Pathways**: Create clear routes for youth to train as lay preachers, worship leaders, or ministry interns.

- **Resource Sharing**: Develop an open-access library of sermons, songs, videos, and prayers created by CCCS members.

- **Ministerial Training Reform**: Encourage theological colleges to integrate cultural competency, bilingual preaching, and youth ministry into core training.

These structures communicate to youth that they are not future leaders – they are today's leaders.

8. A Theology of Hope and Transformation

Underpinning all of this is a theology of transformation. God is not finished with the CCCS. The Spirit is still moving in our communities, still calling new prophets, still planting seeds of renewal.

We must teach a theology that:

- Embraces *fa'asinomaga* (identity) and *agaga* (spirit) as intertwined.

- Understands tradition as a river – not a dam.

- Affirms doubt, struggle, and questioning as part of faith.

- Names justice, reconciliation, and belonging as gospel priorities.

This theology will give youth a solid foundation and a reason to stay. It will root them in love, not just law.

9. The Invitation to Begin Today

The future is not a distant dream. It is shaped by what we do next Sunday, next planning meeting, next youth gathering. Ministers and leaders do not need to have all the answers. But we must be willing to start.

Ask one young person to preach with you. Translate one sermon into bilingual format. Invite a group to redesign one worship service. Host one intergenerational *talanoa*. Film one short youth devotional. Listen, reflect, experiment. Then do it again.

Every act of faithfulness – no matter how small – becomes a seed.

Conclusion: Returning to the Heart of the Gospel

Reimagining the church is not about abandoning our roots. It is about returning to the heart of the gospel – a message of radical grace, embodied love, and transforming hope. Jesus did not preserve traditions for their own sake. He fulfilled them by making them breathe.

Our calling is the same. The CCCS is a gift. It has shaped generations. It has taught us to sing, to pray, to orate, to worship. But it is not yet complete. It needs the voices, hearts, and hands of young people to carry it forward.

The future is now. Let us step into it – together. Let us *toe timata le ūpega* once more. And may the Spirit who began this work be faithful to complete it, in every tongue, every generation, and every act of love.

Conclusion: Hope, Faith, and a Net Recast

The journey through these pages has traced both the challenge and promise facing the Congregational Christian Church Samoa (CCCS). We have wrestled with the realities of youth disengagement, the cultural shifts of Samoan life in Aotearoa New Zealand, and the vital role preaching and worship play in shaping identity and sustaining faith. We have been reminded that the pulpit is not a relic of the past, but a living vessel for truth and transformation when guided by the Spirit. The voices of young people – sometimes hesitant, sometimes defiant, often yearning – have echoed throughout this work. Their cries are not against faith, but for a faith that feels like home. Now, as we conclude, we gather the threads of this weaving and ask: what must we do next?

This chapter is a call to all who love the CCCS – ministers, lay leaders, elders, youth, and families – to walk forward together with courage, humility, and hope. The challenge is not small. But neither is the God who calls us.

A Church at the Threshold

In the ancient world, thresholds were sacred. They marked the crossing from one space to another – from the known to the unknown, from the safe to the risky. The CCCS now stands at such a threshold. It can remain within the house it has known – shaped by its history, language, and liturgical rhythm. Or it can step into a space of transformation, where these same traditions are reimagined in dialogue with the next generation.

To cross a threshold is not to abandon what is behind, but to carry it with discernment. What do we carry forward? What do we lay down? What new tools might we pick up along the way? These are the questions of a maturing faith community.

Courage as Faith in Action

We often think of courage as boldness – standing firm, speaking up, breaking through. But for the CCCS, courage may look different. It may look like listening. Like relinquishing control. Like letting the youth plan a service that feels unfamiliar to elders. Like preaching in two languages even when it feels awkward. Like embracing questions without rushing to answers.

Courage, in this context, is faith in action. It is trusting that the Spirit who birthed the CCCS in Samoa is also at work in the hearts of its youth in New Zealand. It is trusting that God's purposes are not behind us, but ahead of us.

Faithfulness to the Gospel, Not to Fear

Too often, churches respond to change with fear – fear of decline, of losing identity, of disrespecting elders, of losing theological soundness. These fears are understandable. But they cannot govern our decisions. Faithfulness to the gospel calls us to something greater: to hope, to inclusion, to transformation.

The gospel is not static. It is alive, always becoming flesh in new times and places. For the CCCS, the challenge is not to preserve a moment in history, but to carry the gospel faithfully into a changing world. This is what it means to be an apostolic church – not only in lineage, but in mission.

Tradition as River, Not Dam

Tui Atua Tupua Tamasese Efi reminds us that tradition is not a set of unchanging rules, but a living river. It flows, carrying the wisdom of the past, shaped by each generation that steps into its waters. If we try to dam the river – to freeze tradition in place – we risk stagnation. But if we open pathways, tradition nourishes new life.

This is the heart of reinterpreting tradition. Samoan oratory can still stir hearts – when it speaks to the real lives of its hearers. Preaching can still shape identity – when it builds bridges, not barriers. Worship can still carry the sacred – when it includes the voices of youth as well as elders.

Let tradition be the river that connects generations. Let it carry the stories of ancestors, the questions of youth, and the call of Christ.

The Net We Recast

Throughout this book, the image of *toe timata le ūpega* – recasting the net – has guided our reflections. It is a metaphor of renewal. The net may have torn. The fish may have scattered. But the call remains: cast again.

To recast the net is to begin again, not with despair, but with determination. It is to admit what has not worked and try a new way. It is to gather community and say, "Let's try together." It is to trust that God still fills nets, still calls disciples, still speaks across waves.

In practice, this might look like:

- Creating a bilingual preaching team.
- Running a youth-led creative worship service once a month.
- Holding intergenerational *talanoa* about the future of the church.
- Introducing storytelling and testimony into regular services.
- Encouraging ministers to experiment with series-based preaching that addresses youth concerns.
- Building spiritual mentorship between elders and youth.

These are not radical departures. They are faithful responses.

What's at Stake

What is at stake in this moment is not simply church attendance. It is the transmission of a living faith. If the CCCS does not adapt, it risks becoming a beautiful memory rather than a vibrant movement.

But adaptation is not compromise. It is discipleship. It is learning again how to preach good news. How to tend the sacred space between generations. How to shape worship that builds both *fa'asinomaga* and *agaga*. How to speak the language of God's love in a world of change.

The Seeds Already Growing

There is hope. Already, across New Zealand and elsewhere, some CCCS congregations are finding new ways. There are services where youth lead prayers and play music. There are elders who invite youth into planning. There are preachers experimenting with bilingual sermons. There are worship teams who meet between Sundays to dream, not just to rehearse.

These stories are the seeds of the future. Let them be watered. Let them be shared. Let them grow.

A Shared Journey

No minister can do this alone. No youth leader can carry the church on their back. Renewal is not the job of one committee, or one passionate elder. It is a shared journey.

- **Ministers:** Preach as if your life depended on it. Because the life of the church does.

- **Elders:** Open your hearts to change. Trust that tradition is not being lost – it is being renewed.

- **Youth:** Speak your truth with courage. Your voice matters.

- **Families:** Worship together. Eat together. Share stories of faith in your homes.

Together, we become the body of Christ – not just in form, but in mission.

Casting the Net – Again and Again

Let us return to the shoreline.

The night has passed. The first light glimmers on the water. The nets – worn, perhaps torn – are in our hands.

The call comes again: *Toe timata le ūpega.*

Cast again.

Not because we failed. But because we are faithful.

Cast again.

Not to prove ourselves. But to proclaim the goodness of God.

Cast again.

Because there are still fish in the sea. Still young people longing for meaning. Still a God who calls.

Final Blessing

May the CCCS become a place where preaching enlivens, not dulls. Where worship is a dance between the old and the new. Where youth find not judgment, but joy. Where elders are not feared, but honoured. Where the Spirit is not boxed in, but invited.

May we all have courage to change, humility to listen, and faith to begin again.

With God's help, and our faithfulness, the net can be cast again – and it will hold.

Amene.

Acknowledgements

To my parents the late Maulolo Aiaifua and the late Pu'a Tausili Maulolo, even though you are no longer with us, I treasure you both in my heart. Your encouragement and prayers have moulded me to who I am today. To my siblings and families, and my extended family – my heartfelt gratitude for your constant prayers and support always and in all ways to complete this project successfully.

To my wife's parents – the late Muliaga David and the late Sauimalae Tavita, brothers, sisters and families, thank you also for your prayers and support in many ways.

I would like to express my appreciation to the Congregational Christian Church Samoa and the Elders Committee for your encouragement and prayers.

I would also like to thank the Malua Theological College Principal Rev Professor Vaitusi Nofoaiga, the Faculty and College for your continuous support throughout this project. May God bless you all.

Lastly, I take this opportunity to thank my wife Fuarosa and my two sons Fiso and Simona Maulolo. Your endless support and words of advice enabled me to go the extra mile to complete this project.

God bless and faafetai tele lava.

Glossary of Samoan and theological terms

Agaga　　　　Samoan word for "spirit" – refers to the spiritual essence or soul within a person.

Aiga　　　　Extended family – includes not just immediate family but broader kinship groups in Samoan culture.

Fa'aSamoa　　"The Samoan way" – the cultural values, customs, and social structures that define Samoan identity.

Fa'asinomaga　Samoan term for "identity" – especially one's sense of belonging and connection to people, place, and history.

Hermeneutics　The theory and method of interpreting scripture – how we understand and apply the Bible today.

Lotu　　　　Samoan term for worship or religious devotion. Refers to formal Christian worship and spirituality.

Oratory　　　A formal style of speaking or preaching – in the Samoan context, this includes respectful protocols and metaphor.

Preaching　　The act of proclaiming the Word of God through a sermon – central to CCCS worship.

Talanoa　　　A conversational practice in the Pacific that involves open, respectful storytelling and dialogue, often used for communal decision-making.

Tautua　　　Service – often used to express the cultural and spiritual duty to serve others and the community.

Theology　　The study or understanding of God and divine things – can be academic or rooted in lived faith.

Toe timata le ūpega	A Samoan proverb meaning "recast the net" – a metaphor for trying again, renewing efforts, or starting afresh.
Va	A foundational Samoan concept meaning "relational space" – the sacred space between people, often understood as spiritual, social, and ethical.

Sample Sermon Outlines

Here are six sample sermon outlines or themes designed specifically for youth-oriented services within the CCCS context. Each one integrates biblical content, Samoan cultural values, and the lived realities of young people in Aotearoa New Zealand.

1. Theme: "Where Do I Belong?" – Identity in Christ and Culture

- **Text:** 1 Peter 2:9-10 ("You are a chosen people…")
- **Purpose:** Help youth see themselves as loved, chosen, and valued – in both Samoan and Kiwi contexts.
- **Sermon Flow:**
    - Introduction: The feeling of being caught between two cultures.
    - Scripture unpacked: God gives us identity before the world does.
    - Real-life stories: Identity struggles of NZ-born Samoan youth.
    - Cultural bridge: *Fa'asinomaga* and being *aiga* in God's family.
    - Application: Embrace both identities and find wholeness in Christ.

2. Theme: "God in the Chaos" – Mental Health and Faith

- **Text:** Psalm 46:1-3 ("God is our refuge and strength…")
- **Purpose:** Speak openly about anxiety, depression, and stress as spiritual concerns.
- **Sermon Flow:**
    - Naming the storm: School pressure, family tension, cultural expectations.

- Scripture unpacked: God is present even when everything feels unstable.

- Testimony: Invite a young person to share a struggle and how God met them.

- Samoan values: Normalising emotional honesty as strength (*fa'amaoni* – truthfulness).

- Application: Finding hope, help, and healing in church, Scripture, and one another.

3. Theme: "What's the Point of Church?" – Reclaiming Purpose

- **Text:** Acts 2:42-47 (The early church as a vibrant, living community)
- **Purpose:** Help youth reimagine church not as a routine, but as a movement.
- **Sermon Flow:**
  - Challenge: Why do so many youth see church as boring or irrelevant?
  - Scripture unpacked: The first Christians built a shared life, not just services.
  - Illustration: Modern-day youth-led service examples.
  - Cultural insight: *Tautua* (service) as spiritual calling.
  - Application: What kind of church would make you excited to come?

4. Theme: "Speak Life" – Words That Heal, Not Hurt

- **Text:** Proverbs 18:21 ("The tongue has the power of life and death...")
- **Purpose:** Address issues of bullying, gossip, online shaming, and verbal abuse.

- **Sermon Flow:**
  - Hook: Screenshots last forever – so do wounds from words.
  - Scripture unpacked: Words build up or destroy – what kind of speaker are you?
  - Storytelling: Contrast between hurtful and healing conversations.
  - Samoan wisdom: The sacredness of *upu* (words) and oratory.
  - Application: Create a community where young people speak life to one another.

5. Theme: "Faith in Action" – Not Just Hearing, But Doing

- **Text:** James 2:14–7 ("Faith without works is dead.")
- **Purpose:** Encourage youth to live out faith in tangible ways.
- **Sermon Flow:**
  - Setup: "I believe in God" – but what does that look like Monday to Saturday?
  - Scripture unpacked: Active faith is real faith.
  - Examples: Youth-led outreach, climate justice, helping elders.
  - Samoan value: *Tautua loto faamaoni* (service from a sincere heart).
  - Challenge: What can you do this week to put faith into action?

6. Theme: "God Hears You" – Prayer and Connection in Daily Life

- **Text:** Philippians 4:6-7 ("Do not be anxious about anything…")
- **Purpose:** Teach youth that prayer is simple, powerful, and personal.
- **Sermon Flow:**
  - Story: "I don't know how to pray" – common youth comment.
  - Scripture unpacked: Prayer is conversation, not performance.

- Visuals: Break down prayer into images – text message, voice note, breath.

- Samoan theology: God as *Tamā alofa* – loving parent who listens.

- Practice: End with a short guided prayer experience or journaling.

Group Discussion Questions

Here are 20 group discussion questions tailored for ministerial retreats, lay leadership training, or parish planning groups in the context of the CCCS. These questions aim to provoke honest reflection, generate constructive dialogue, and inspire practical action – especially in relation to youth engagement, preaching renewal, and intergenerational transformation.

1: Preaching and Relevance

- What makes a sermon meaningful or memorable to you personally?

- How can we tell when preaching is connecting – or failing to connect – with our youth?

- What are the risks of changing how we preach? What are the risks of not changing?

- How can we retain the richness of Samoan oratory while also making sermons accessible to New Zealand-born listeners?

2: Youth Engagement

- What do our young people need from church that they are not currently receiving?

- In what ways are our current worship services welcoming – or unwelcoming – to youth?

- How can we encourage youth to participate more actively in planning and leading worship?

- What stops us from giving young people real responsibility or leadership in church life?

3: Cultural and Generational Tension

- Where do we see tension between Samoan traditions and New Zealand realities?

- How can we hold on to our Samoan values while making space for change?

- What role should bilingual language play in worship and preaching?

- How do we ensure respect for elders while also empowering youth to speak and lead?

4: Reimagining Church

- What would our ideal CCCS congregation look like in 10 years?

- What new forms of worship or service have you seen elsewhere that could work in our context?

- How do we move from being a church that preserves tradition to a church that *grows* tradition?

- What does a vibrant, Spirit-led, intergenerational church feel like? What does it sound like?

5: Leadership and Change

- How can ministers and lay leaders model courage and humility during times of change?

- What fears do we need to name and release in order to move forward as a church?

- What would it look like to *toe timata le ūpega* (recast the net) in our own congregation?

- What one small, faithful step can we take this month to bridge the gap between generations?

Key Interview Insights

Here are anonymised reflections from youth, elders, and ministers across CCCS congregations in Aotearoa New Zealand.

1. Youth Voices – Honest, Hopeful, Frustrated

Language barriers are real.
- "It's not that I don't care about the sermon – I just don't know what most of it means."
- "Sometimes I look at my parents and pretend to understand, but I'm lost."
- "When the preacher uses a few words in English, I suddenly feel like I'm invited into the message."

Worship often feels disconnected.
- "Church is beautiful, but it doesn't feel like it's for me."
- "We go because we're expected to, but we leave with more questions than answers."
- "The way church is run makes me feel like an outsider in my own culture."

Desire for authenticity and participation.
- "Don't just ask us to sing or read scripture once a year – invite us into decisions."
- "Let us be part of the planning, not just the performance."
- "I'd love to help shape a service that speaks to mental health, identity, and God."

Not rejecting faith – seeking relevance.
- "I still pray. I still believe. But I don't know how my faith connects with my life right now."

- "I don't need answers to everything. I just want to know God is still with me."

- "We're not trying to rebel. We just want faith that speaks our language – spiritually and literally."

Open to change – if leaders are.

- "If our ministers really asked what we think, we'd tell them. But they never ask."

- "I've seen one church do youth-led worship – it was amazing. I wish our church would try."

- "It would mean the world if our elders just came to one youth meeting and listened."

2. Elders' Voices – Proud, Concerned, Cautious

Pride in tradition and sacred responsibility.

- "We've kept this faith alive through generations. That is no small thing."

- "The *faifeʻau* is chosen by God. The way he preaches should not be taken lightly."

- "Our ways are not random – they are rooted in respect, theology, and culture."

Concern about loss of respect and identity.

- "In the name of modernisation, we must not lose our sense of who we are."

- "The young ones today don't always show *faʻaaloalo*. We fear what comes next."

- "If we change everything, will it still be the CCCS? Or just another youth club?"

Acknowledgement that change is needed – but fear of losing control.

- "Yes, they must be included. But there is a way. A process. Not chaos."

- "Innovation is not bad. But who decides what changes, and how?"
- "We are open to new things, but not to losing what we've faithfully built."

Appreciation for spiritual formation – not just performance.

- "Youth must not only know how to speak – they must know whom they speak of."
- "Let them lead, yes, but let them be discipled first."
- "We need depth – not just energy and emotion."

Concern for legacy and future.

- "We do all this for them. But will they carry it on?"
- "Sometimes I cry at night – I see empty pews and wonder, will the CCCS survive here?"
- "I don't want to die knowing the church didn't listen to its young."

3. Ministers' Voices – Tired, Visionary, Torn

Preaching is seen as core, but hard to adapt.

- "This is the ministry we inherited. Change feels like betrayal sometimes."
- "It's difficult – I want to preach so all can hear, but also honour the richness of Samoan oratory."
- "The younger generation wants storytelling, visuals, honesty. I wasn't trained for that."

Feel pressure from both sides.

- "Elders ask why we're softening the gospel. Youth ask why we don't make it relevant. It's hard."
- "Everyone wants something different. Sometimes I feel like I can't win."

- "We're caught between generations. We carry both their hopes and their frustrations."

Long for deeper engagement and partnership.

- "Youth are hungry for meaning – they're not lazy, they're just not fed properly."

- "Elders are not against youth – they just fear losing what they love."

- "We need to bring them together, not just manage them separately."

Some are quietly innovating.

- "We tried testimonies during Lent – the youth responded deeply."

- "One month we preached on topics like belonging, anxiety, and God's voice – attendance rose."

- "I used English metaphors and Samoan proverbs side by side – it worked."

Need for support, training, and trust.

- "We need spaces to reimagine ministry together, not just defend tradition."

- "I sometimes feel alone – like change is up to me, and I'll be blamed either way."

- "Give us permission to experiment. To learn. To fail and try again."

Common Themes Across All Groups

Theme	Insight
Language	Preaching in Samoan holds sacred meaning but often loses youth. Bilingual approaches (Samoan-English) offer promise for comprehension and inclusion.
Relevance	Youth seek messages addressing real-life issues: identity, belonging, mental health, peer pressure, school, and hope. Adults worry about theology being "watered down."
Respect	Youth feel silenced. Elders feel dishonoured. Ministers feel stuck. All express a desire for mutual respect and safe dialogue.
Preaching	Youth value clarity, passion, and connection. Elders value dignity, structure, and theological authority. Ministers are beginning to explore new forms.
Worship	Youth want variety – music, media, movement. Elders want continuity. Some churches are experimenting with intergenerational collaboration.
Participation	Young people want real roles, not tokenism. Elders want youth to understand church first. Ministers are looking for pathways to bridge both.
Identity	Many youth feel "caught between cultures" and want preaching that validates their experience. Preaching can be key in affirming both *fa'asinomaga* and *agaga*.
Hope	Despite tensions, all voices express a deep love for the church and desire to see it thrive into the future.

Bibliography and Suggested Reading List

Theology and Ministry in Oceania

- Havea, Jione. *Island Churches: Challenge and Change*. Suva: Institute for Research and Social Analysis, 2001.

- Havea, Jione (ed). *Indigenous Australia and the Unfinished Business of Theology: Cross-Cultural Engagement*. Postcolonialism and Religions series. Palgrave Macmillan, 2014.

- Tofaeono, Ama'amalele. *Eco-Theology: Aiga – The Household of Life*. Apia: PICTS, 2000.

- Halapua, Winston. *Tradition, Lotu & Militarism in Fiji*. Lautoka: Fiji Institute of Applied Studies, 2003.

- Lalomauga, Filoimea Telisa. *Preaching from the Pacific Pulpit: The Samoan Context and Christian Ministry*. Apia: Malua Theological College, 2012.

Samoan Culture and Identity

- Tamasese, Tui Atua Tupua. *In Search of Meaning, Nuance and Metaphor in Social Policy*. Suva: University of the South Pacific, 2008.

- Tamasese, Tui Atua Tupua. *Clutter in Samoan Theology: Towards a Respectful Samoan Spirituality*. Public Lecture, University of Otago, 2005.

- Tamasailau Suaalii-Sauni et al. (eds). *Su'esu'e Manogi: In Search of Fragrance – Tui Atua Tupua Tamasese Ta'isi and the Samoan Indigenous Reference*. Apia: National University of Samoa, 2009.

- Va'ai, Upolu Luma. *Fa'amata'i and Social Welfare: A Theological Exploration of the Fa'amata'i and the Role of the Church in Addressing Poverty.* Suva: PTC Education by Extension, 2001.

- Anae, Melani. *Pacific Identities and Well-Being: Cross-Cultural Perspectives.* Dunedin: Otago University Press, 2016.

- Le Tagaloa, Aiono Fanaafi. *O Motuga'afa – Selected Writings of Aiono Fanaafi Le Tagaloa.* Apia: Le Lamepa Press, 1996.

Youth, Diaspora, and Cultural Change

- Macpherson, Cluny & Macpherson, La'avasa. *The Warm Winds of Change: Globalisation in Contemporary Samoa.* Auckland: Auckland University Press, 2009.

- Tupuola, Anne-Marie. *Learning Sexuality: Young Samoan Women.* Suva: Institute of Pacific Studies, 2004.

- Tanielu, R. & Johnson, A. *This Is Home: A Study on the State of Pasifika People in New Zealand 2021.* Auckland: The Salvation Army Social Policy Unit, 2021.

- Koloto, Alisi, et al. *Pacific Youth in New Zealand: Aspirations and Realities.* Wellington: Ministry of Youth Affairs, 2006.

Preaching, Worship and Liturgical Innovation

- Long, Thomas G. *The Witness of Preaching.* Louisville: Westminster John Knox Press, 2005.

- Allen, Ronald J. *Preaching the Topical Sermon.* Louisville: Westminster John Knox Press, 1992.

- Taylor, Barbara Brown. *The Preaching Life.* Cowley Publications, 1993.

- Walton, Jonathan L. *Watch This! The Ethics and Aesthetics of Black Televangelism.* New York: NYU Press, 2009.

- Tisdale, Leonora Tubbs. *Prophetic Preaching: A Pastoral Approach.* Louisville: Westminster John Knox Press, 2010.

- Lathrop, Gordon W. *Holy Things: A Liturgical Theology.* Minneapolis: Fortress Press, 1993.

Pacific Hermeneutics and Indigenous Methodologies

- Smith, Linda Tuhiwai. *Decolonizing Methodologies: Research and Indigenous Peoples*. London: Zed Books, 1999.

- Nabobo-Baba, Unaisi. *Knowing and Learning: An Indigenous Fijian Approach*. Suva: University of the South Pacific, 2006.

- Va'ai, Upolu Luma & Casimira, Anapesi (eds). *Religious and Cultural Values: Reweaving the Ecological Mat*. Suva: Pacific Theological College, 2017.

- Fonoti, Makere. *Tagata o le Moana: Reflections from Oceania*. Auckland: AUT Pacific Media Centre, 2011.

Recommended for Church Study Groups or Retreats

- Nofoaiga, Vaitusi. *A Samoan Reading of Discipleship in Matthew*. Atlanta, Georgia: SBL Press, 2017.

- Pouono, Terry. "Indigenous Language Loss: The Future of Gagana Samoa (Samoan Language) in Diaspora" In *Postcolonial Voices from Downunder*, ed. Jione Havea, 170-181. Eugene, Oregon: Pickwick Publications, 2017

- Matapo Jacob and Dion Enari, D. (2021). Re-imagining the dialogic spaces of talanoa through Samoan ontoepistemology. *Waikato Journal of Education. Special Issue: Talanoa Va: Honouring Pacific Research and Online Engagement*, 26, 79-88. https://wje.org.nz/index.php/WJE/article/view/770/682

- Dreyer, Yolanda. *Practical Theology: A Theology of Interdisciplinarity*. University of Pretoria, 2004.

- Padilla, C. René. *Mission Between the Times: Essays on the Kingdom*. Langham, 2010.